Belief, Fear, and Love

The Brutal Truth of How I Have Learned All Three of These Have Shaped Our Lives and Choices

Ron Moncrief

Copyright © 2024 Trient Press

All rights reserved. No portion of this publication may be reproduced, distributed, or transmitted in any form or by any means, including photocopying, recording, or other electronic or mechanical methods, without the prior written permission of the publisher. This restriction excludes brief quotations utilized in critical reviews and certain other noncommercial usages as permitted by copyright law. For permission inquiries, direct correspondence to the publisher, marked "Attention: Permissions Coordinator," at the following address:

Trient Press
5470 Kietzke Lane Suite 300 - #394
Reno, NV 89511

Criminal copyright infringement, including instances without financial gain, is subject to investigation by the FBI and incurs penalties of up to five years in federal imprisonment and a fine of $250,000.
Excepting the original narrative material authored by Ron Moncrief, all songs, song titles, and lyrics cited within Belief, Fear, and Love remain the exclusive property of their respective artists, songwriters, and copyright holders.

Ordering Information:
For quantity sales, Trient Press offers special discounts to corporations, associations, and other organizations. For detailed information, contact the publisher at the address provided above.
For orders by U.S. trade bookstores and wholesalers, please reach out to
Trient Press at Tel: (775) 996-3844, or visit www.trientpress.com.
Printed in the United States of America
Publisher's Cataloging-in-Publication Data
Moncrief, Ron
Belief, Fear, and Love
Paperback: ISBN 979-8-88990-188-4
E-Book: 979-8-88990-189-1

Prologue

In my years as a coach, I've come to understand that belief, fear, and love aren't just emotions or states of mind. They're the architects of our reality, the unseen hands that sculpt the clay of our lives. As I've navigated through the ups and downs of coaching women's basketball, these three forces have revealed themselves in countless ways, shaping not only my journey but also the paths of the young women I've had the privilege to mentor.

Belief: The Foundation of Our Reality

Belief is like a lens. It colors how we see the world, influencing our interpretation of every event, every interaction. In my early coaching days, I saw belief work its magic in the most unexpected ways. A player who believed she could outjump her opponent often did, not because she suddenly gained more muscle, but because her belief shaped her reality. She saw opportunities where others saw obstacles. Her belief wasn't just a feeling; it was a powerful force that transformed her perception and, consequently, her actions.

I remember a game where we were trailing by a significant margin at halftime. The locker room was heavy with defeat, the air thick with disbelief. That's when I realized my most important job as a coach wasn't just to teach basketball skills; it was to cultivate belief. I looked at my team, a group of young women who had worked tirelessly all season, and said, "Believe not in the scoreboard, but in your ability to change it." It wasn't just a pep talk; it was a call to shift their perception.

What happened in the second half was nothing short of miraculous. The team that walked back onto the court wasn't the same one that had left it. Their belief had reshaped their reality. They played with a ferocity and confidence that was absent in the first half. We didn't just close the gap; we won the game. It was a clear demonstration of how belief can alter our reality, turning the impossible into the possible.

As a young Black coach, belief has been my compass, guiding me through a landscape often riddled with doubts and stereotypes. I've learned to see belief as more than just a feeling; it's a tool, a strategy, a way of life. It's about seeing beyond the immediate, beyond the conventional wisdom and the naysayers. Belief is what pushes you when everything else is pulling you back.

In my journey, I've seen belief act as a bridge over the chasm of fear and uncertainty. It has been the light in the darkest of times, illuminating paths that were invisible to the eyes clouded by doubt. Belief is the foundation upon which we build our lives, the bedrock that holds firm even when everything else is shifting. It's the lens through which we see not just what is, but what could be.

As I share my story, remember this: your belief is your most powerful asset. It's the force that can shape your world, redefine your reality, and rewrite the rules of the game. In the game of life, just like in basketball, it's not just about what you can do; it's about what you believe you can do. This understanding has been the cornerstone of my coaching philosophy and, more importantly, my life philosophy. Belief, in its purest form, is the genesis of all we dare to dream and all we dare to achieve.

The Power of Self-Fulfilling Prophecies

As I reflect on my journey, one fundamental truth stands out - the power of self-fulfilling prophecies in shaping our lives. This phenomenon, where our expectations and beliefs carve out our future, is not just psychological jargon; it's a tangible force, as real and potent as any strategy I've employed on the basketball court.

Picture this: a player walks onto the court, shoulders slumped, eyes filled with the shadow of doubt. She's already lost the game in her mind. Her belief, or the lack thereof, sets a prophecy in motion. Each missed shot reinforces her belief. "I can't do this," she whispers to herself. And the universe consents. But, what if she believed otherwise? What if her inner narrative was one of strength, not surrender? This shift in belief doesn't just change her attitude; it alters the outcome. Her shots find their mark, her defense becomes impenetrable, not because of a sudden influx of skill, but because her belief has authored a new reality.

In coaching, I've seen this time and again. The team that believes in their victory fights harder, plays smarter, and often, emerges victorious. It's not magic; it's the power of belief manifesting as a self-fulfilling prophecy. It's about writing your story before it unfolds on the court.

This principle extends far beyond basketball. In life, we are often the authors of our own narratives. The beliefs we hold about ourselves and our potential orchestrate the outcomes we experience. Believing that you're capable, worthy, and destined for greatness isn't an act of arrogance; it's an act of creation. You're setting the stage, scripting the play of your life.

But, it's crucial to acknowledge the shadow side of this power. Negative beliefs can just as easily manifest negative outcomes. The belief that you're doomed to fail, that you're unworthy of success, or that happiness is for others, not you, can set you on a path of self-destruction. In my coaching career, part of my job has been to help players dismantle these destructive beliefs, to show them that they are not bound by the limitations they've set for themselves.

I've had to confront my own set of limiting beliefs, born out of societal stereotypes and personal insecurities. There were moments when I doubted my ability, questioned my worth, and feared I wouldn't measure up. But, with time, I've learned to rewrite my internal script, to believe in my power to shape my destiny. This shift in belief has been my greatest victory, greater than any championship I've won.

Remember this: Your beliefs set the stage for your life's play. They are not just passive thoughts; they are active creators of your reality. Choose them wisely, for they have the power to craft your destiny. As you turn the pages of this book, and of your life, be mindful of the prophecies you're writing with each belief you hold. Your story is yours to write; make it one of triumph, not tragedy.

Transformation through Belief

I've witnessed remarkable transformations, not just in skills on the court, but in the hearts and minds of the players I've mentored. These transformations have one common denominator: a shift in belief. The fluid and dynamic nature of belief systems is not just a philosophical concept; it's a lived reality, one that I've seen unfold in real-time, on and off the court.

I remember a player, let's call her Kayla. Kayla came to our team with raw talent but burdened by a belief that she was 'just average'. This belief had become her reality. She played safe, never pushing beyond her comfort zone. Her transformation began the day we sat down and talked about her beliefs. "What if you're more than average?" I asked. "What if you're extraordinary waiting to be discovered?" This conversation sparked a change in Kayla. It wasn't overnight, but it was profound.

As her belief about herself changed, so did her performance. She started to take risks, to play with a boldness that was absent before. The most remarkable transformation was in her eyes – they now sparkled with the belief that she could be whoever she wanted to be, on and off the court. Kayla's story is a testament to the power of belief in catalyzing personal transformation.

Another story that comes to mind is of our team facing a seemingly unbeatable opponent. The general belief was that we stood no chance. I saw this as an opportunity to challenge and change our collective belief. "Why not us?" I challenged them. "Why can't we be the David to their Goliath?" Gradually, the belief within the team shifted. We went into the game as underdogs but left as victors. It wasn't just a win in the record books; it was a win over our limiting beliefs.

These stories illustrate the dynamic nature of belief. It's not static; it evolves as we feed it new experiences, perspectives, and reflections. In coaching, I've learned to treat belief as a malleable substance, something that can be shaped and reshaped to unlock potential, to overcome barriers, and to transform lives.

As I pen down these experiences, my aim is not just to narrate stories from the basketball court. It's to highlight a fundamental truth of human existence - our beliefs define us, but they don't have to confine us. They are the starting point, not the end. The belief that you start with is not the belief you need to carry forever. It can change, grow, and evolve, just as you do.

The takeaway from these reflections is clear: be mindful of your beliefs, for they are the architects of your destiny. Challenge them, grow them, and when necessary, change them. Your beliefs are your most potent allies in the journey of life. Use them wisely, and watch as they transform the impossible into the possible, the average into the extraordinary, the dream into reality.

As you read on, consider your own beliefs. Are they serving you, or are they holding you back? Remember, the power to transform your life lies within you, in your ability to believe in the beauty of your dreams and the power of your potential.

The Unseen Architects - Belief, Fear, and Love

Finally, I've learned that belief, fear, and love are more than mere emotions; they are the unseen architects shaping the very essence of our lives. They sculpt the clay of our existence, molding our perceptions, our actions, and ultimately, our destinies. Throughout my journey in coaching women's basketball, I have witnessed firsthand how these powerful forces influence not only my path but also the lives of the young athletes I've had the honor to guide.

Belief has been the foundation, the lens through which we perceive our world. It's fascinating how belief can transform reality, turning what seems impossible into the possible. I've seen players overcome insurmountable odds simply because they believed they could. It's not just about instilling basketball skills; it's about nurturing the belief in one's abilities, in one's potential. This belief isn't a mere emotion; it's a force that reshapes perception and action.

The power of self-fulfilling prophecies further underscores this concept. Belief, or the lack thereof, sets a trajectory for success or failure. I've observed players defeat themselves before the game even starts, their disbelief manifesting in their performance. Conversely, those who step onto the court with a conviction of victory often create their desired outcome. Belief is not just a thought; it's an active creator of reality.

But belief's power isn't confined to the basketball court. It extends to every facet of life, where our beliefs about ourselves and our capabilities dictate the outcomes we experience. Holding onto beliefs of capability and worth can lead to triumph, while succumbing to beliefs of inadequacy and failure can lead to defeat. As a coach, part of my role has been to dismantle these limiting beliefs, to illuminate the potential that lies within each player.

This journey has also been a personal one, where I've had to confront and reshape my own beliefs, especially those shaped by societal stereotypes and personal insecurities. Rewriting this internal script has been my greatest victory, far surpassing any championship title.

The stories of transformation through belief that I've witnessed are a testament to its fluid and dynamic nature. Belief is not static; it evolves with our experiences and reflections. I've seen players, initially shackled by self-doubt, transform into confident, assertive individuals. This malleability of belief is a powerful tool, capable of unlocking potential, overcoming barriers, and inducing profound personal transformations.

As you delve into the pages that follow, I invite you to reflect on your own beliefs. Are they serving as bridges to your goals, or barriers hindering your path? Remember, the power to transform your life resides in your beliefs. Embrace them, challenge them, and when necessary, change them. Your beliefs are the compass guiding you through the journey of life. Use them to navigate toward your dreams, and watch as they transform the seemingly impossible into your reality.

Fear - The Barrier to Our Potential

Chapter 1

As I reflect on my journey, not just as a coach but as a man who has seen life's many seasons, I realize the undeniable impact of fear. Fear, in its many forms, has often stood as a towering barrier to potential, not only in the lives of the athletes I've coached but in my own life as well. Understanding and confronting this formidable opponent has been a central theme in my coaching philosophy and personal growth.

Fear is a paradox. It's both a protector and a captor. On the basketball court, I've seen fear in the eyes of players facing a formidable opponent or taking a crucial shot. This fear can protect them, making them cautious and strategic, but more often, it becomes a chain that binds their true potential. It whispers tales of failure, of judgment, of not being good enough. And in listening to these whispers, players, and indeed all of us, limit the heights we can reach.

My experience has shown me that fear, while universal, is also deeply personal. As a young Black man in America, my fears were compounded by societal perceptions and stereotypes. There were times when these fears seemed to overshadow my abilities and aspirations. It took me years to understand that the fear within me was not just an enemy to be fought, but a voice to be understood and challenged.

In coaching, I've often played the role of a guide, helping my players navigate through their fears. There's a story that stands out in my mind. There was a player, immensely talented, but her fear of failure was like a shadow that followed her on and off the court. Her fear was rooted in a deep-seated belief that she wasn't good enough, a belief that was reinforced by every missed shot and every lost game. My challenge was to help her see fear not as a wall blocking her path, but as a hurdle to be jumped over. We worked not just on her skills with the ball, but on her mindset, her internal dialogue. Slowly, she started to see fear as a signal, a sign that she was pushing beyond her comfort zone, stepping into new territories. Her transformation was not immediate, but it was profound.

This journey of understanding fear is not just for athletes; it's for everyone. Fear has a way of creeping into our lives, shaping our decisions, our relationships, our careers. It can be subtle, a quiet voice of doubt, or loud, a thunderous roar of anxiety. But in every form, it limits our potential.

The key to overcoming fear is not in silencing it, but in listening to it, understanding it, and then moving beyond it. Fear often points to what matters to us, to the dreams we cherish, and the goals we aspire to achieve. By facing our fears, we not only confront what scares us but also affirm what we value.

As I write these words, I want you to think about the fears that have held you back. What are they protecting you from? What are they keeping you captive from? Remember, fear is not the enemy; it's a signpost, directing you to the areas where growth is waiting. Embrace your fears, understand them, and then dare to move past them. On the other side of fear lies the untapped potential, the unexplored territory of your true capabilities.

Fear as a Protective Mechanism

I've come to understand fear in its dual role: as a guardian and a jailer. It's important to acknowledge that fear, in its essence, is a natural protective mechanism. It's an evolutionary gift, wired into us to keep us safe from harm. On the court, I've seen fear serve as a shield, prompting players to be more alert, more aware of their surroundings. This kind of fear can be a positive force, a necessary caution in the face of real dangers.

However, the challenge arises when this protective mechanism becomes an overbearing influence, morphing into a barrier that shackles us. This transformation of fear from a protector to a captor is subtle yet profound. It starts as a small voice of caution but can quickly amplify into a chorus of doubts, paralyzing us from taking action. It's like having an overprotective parent who, in their desire to keep you safe, ends up stifling your growth.

In my own journey, I've had to wrestle with this overbearing aspect of fear. Growing up as a young Black man and evolving into a coach, fear often presented itself as a daunting barrier. The fear of making a wrong decision, the fear of not living up to expectations, the fear of failure - these fears, while initially protective, gradually began to erode my sense of possibility. They clouded my vision, not allowing me to see beyond the immediate risks to the potential rewards.

The same phenomenon occurs in the lives of the players I coach. I remember one particular player who was exceptionally skilled but was held back by her fear of making mistakes. This fear, initially a form of protection from errors, had grown into a significant barrier, preventing her from taking necessary risks on the court. It was as if her protective gear had become too heavy, hindering her movements instead of safeguarding them.

This is where the delicate balance comes into play. Recognizing fear as a protective mechanism is crucial, but so is realizing when it starts to become a limiting factor. The art lies in distinguishing between legitimate caution and irrational fear. In coaching, I strive to help my players understand this difference. We work on recognizing when fear is serving a useful purpose and when it's merely an echo of outdated anxieties.

To overcome the overbearing aspect of fear, we need to cultivate a mindset that acknowledges fear but is not dominated by it. It involves understanding the roots of our fears, confronting them, and ultimately, learning to manage them. This process isn't about eradicating fear entirely - that's neither possible nor desirable. Instead, it's about developing a relationship with fear where it informs but doesn't control our actions.

As you read these lines, consider your relationship with fear. Is it acting as a shield, or has it become a chain? Learning to navigate this landscape of fear is a lifelong journey. It requires patience, introspection, and the courage to confront what scares us. Remember, on the other side of fear lies a realm of untapped potential and unexplored possibilities. By understanding and managing our fears, we open the door to a world where we are no longer captives, but masters of our own destiny.

The Paralyzing Effect of Fear

In the realm of basketball and life, the paralyzing effect of fear is a phenomenon I have encountered repeatedly. Fear, when it grips the mind, can freeze the most talented athlete in their tracks, turning opportunities into insurmountable obstacles. It's like a thick fog that clouds judgment, blurs vision, and numbs the senses. This paralysis is not just a physical phenomenon; it's deeply psychological, affecting decision-making, creating anxiety, and often preventing us from seizing the opportunities that life presents.

I recall a playoff game, a moment where everything was on the line. One of my players, who had always been the cornerstone of the team, froze under the weight of fear. The fear of losing, the fear of disappointing, the fear of not being perfect. It wasn't just her body that was paralyzed; it was her mind. Every decision was second-guessed, every move was hesitated. The fluidity and grace that defined her game were replaced by rigidity and uncertainty. This paralysis is a testament to fear's power to constrict our natural talents and instincts.

Fear-induced paralysis is not limited to the basketball court. It infiltrates all aspects of life. How many times have we found ourselves at a crossroads, unable to make a decision because of the fear of what lies ahead? How often have we let opportunities slip through our fingers because the fear of failure was more overwhelming than the prospect of success? This paralysis is a silent thief, stealing away possibilities and potentials, often without us even realizing it.

The key to overcoming this paralysis lies in understanding the roots of our fear. It's about dissecting the fear, breaking it down into its components, and confronting them head-on. In coaching, this means creating an environment where failure is not seen as a catastrophe but as a learning opportunity. It's about encouraging players to take calculated risks, to embrace the possibility of failure as a stepping stone to success.

In life, this approach translates to cultivating a mindset of resilience. It's about viewing fear not as a stop sign but as a caution sign, one that advises carefulness but doesn't necessitate a halt. It involves recognizing that the path to success is often littered with failures and that avoiding risk is often the biggest risk of all.

As you continue to read, reflect on how fear has played a role in your life. Has it been a protector, a captor, or both? How has it shaped your decisions, your actions, your path? Remember, the journey to overcoming fear is not about becoming fearless; it's about learning to fear less. It's about understanding that on the other side of fear lies a world of possibilities, waiting to be explored and conquered. Embrace this journey, for it is in confronting our fears that we discover our true potential and strength.

Overcoming Fear: A Path to Liberation and Growth

The moments when I have guided players, and myself, through the labyrinth of fear have been the most transformative. These experiences have taught me that facing and conquering fears is not just about surmounting a challenge; it's about embracing liberation and growth.

One particular instance stands out vividly in my mind. We were facing a critical match, and one of our key players was visibly trembling with fear. This was more than just pre-game jitters; it was a deep-seated fear of failure that had haunted her for seasons. Together, we embarked on a journey of confronting this fear. We started with acknowledging it, not as a weakness but as a part of her human experience.

We then worked on reframing her perspective, helping her understand that failure is not the opposite of success but a part of it.

This process was neither quick nor easy. It involved many conversations, on and off the court. We delved into her past experiences, unraveling the threads of fear that had woven into her psyche. Gradually, she began to see that her fear of failure was based on a narrative that she had the power to rewrite. On the day of the match, she stepped onto the court, not free from fear, but no longer paralyzed by it. Her performance was not flawless, but it was fearless. And that made all the difference.

My own journey with fear has mirrored this process. As a coach, I've faced the fear of not living up to expectations, of making wrong decisions that could cost games, and more importantly, impact the lives of my players. Overcoming these fears has been about embracing them as part of my growth. It's been about understanding that fear is a natural response to the unknown and the unpredictable, but it shouldn't dictate my actions.

The liberation that comes from facing and conquering fears is palpable. It's like breaking free from invisible shackles. This liberation opens up a new realm of possibilities, allowing us to explore paths we might have otherwise shunned. It fosters growth, not just as athletes or professionals, but as individuals. Each time we confront a fear, we emerge stronger, more resilient, and more in tune with our capabilities.

As you navigate through your own fears, remember that the journey of overcoming them is as important as the destination. Each step you take in confronting your fears is a step towards your growth. It's about transforming the energy of fear into the fuel for your journey. Embrace this process, for on the other side of fear lies a version of you that's more capable, more confident, and more complete.

I urge you to view your fears not as insurmountable walls but as hurdles that can be crossed. Overcoming fear is not about the absence of fear; it's about mastering it. It's about taking control of the narrative and turning what once held you back into a force that propels you forward. This is the essence of growth, the crux of liberation, and the heart of true victory.

Confronting the Shadows - Navigating Through Fear

Fear, in its multifaceted nature, often emerges as a formidable barrier, impeding the potential of not only the athletes I've coached but also my own. The essence of this journey has been about understanding fear, engaging with it, and learning to navigate through its shadowy terrains.

Fear is an intricate paradox; it's a protector that can transform into a captor. On the basketball court, fear is visible in the wary eyes of players, facing a tough opponent or making a critical decision. This fear, while sometimes a guardian, often morphs into chains that bind and restrict true potential. It speaks in hushed tones of doubt, failure, and inadequacy. In heeding these whispers, we, as players and individuals, inadvertently limit our horizons.

This experience of fear is universal yet deeply personal. My journey, especially as a young Black coach in America, has been punctuated with fears amplified by societal perceptions and stereotypes. There have been moments where these fears seemed to overshadow my talents and aspirations. Understanding and redefining the fear within has been a pivotal aspect of my growth.

In my role as a coach, guiding players through their fears has been a recurring and transformative theme. The story of a player, paralyzed by the fear of failure, highlights this. Her journey from seeing fear as an insurmountable wall to a hurdle to be cleared, mirrors the journey of self-growth that fear can initiate.

Fear infiltrates all facets of life, influencing decisions, relationships, and career paths. Its manifestation can range from a subtle undertone of doubt to an overwhelming roar of anxiety. In each form, fear curtails potential and possibility.

The art of overcoming fear is not in silencing it but in understanding and transcending it. Fear often highlights what is truly important to us, our cherished dreams, and our sought-after goals. By confronting our fears, we not only challenge what frightens us but also affirm our values and aspirations.

As you ponder over these words, consider the fears that have hindered you. What have they protected you from? What have they prevented you from achieving? Fear, remember, is not an adversary; it's a signpost, guiding you towards areas ripe for growth. Embrace your fears, decipher them, and then boldly step beyond them. Beyond the realm of fear lies untapped potential and uncharted territories of your true capabilities.

Fear, initially a protective mechanism, can become an overpowering force that confines and constricts. Recognizing when fear shifts from being a shield to a shackle is crucial. In my journey, both personally and as a coach, striking a balance between heedful caution and irrational fear has been pivotal. This balance is essential in navigating the landscape of fear, transforming it from a limiting force to a guiding light.

The paralyzing effect of fear is a reality in sports and life. It can freeze the most talented, turning opportunities into impassable hurdles. Overcoming this paralysis involves dissecting fear, understanding its roots, and confronting it head-on. In coaching, this means fostering an environment where failure is a part of learning and growth.

The liberation and growth that come from facing and conquering fears are profound. It's akin to breaking free from invisible chains, opening up new realms of possibilities. This liberation fosters growth, not just professionally but personally. Each encounter with fear is an opportunity for strength, resilience, and self-discovery.

I invite you to view your fears not as insurmountable obstacles but as challenges to be overcome. Mastering fear is not about its eradication; it's about understanding and controlling its influence. This mastery is the essence of growth, the key to liberation, and the heart of true victory. In the journey of overcoming fear, we find our true strength and unlock our fullest potential.

Love - The Ultimate Driving Force

Chapter 2

I've come to recognize love as the most potent, transformative force in our lives. It's a force that transcends mere emotion, shaping our actions, our beliefs, and our destinies in profound ways. As a coach, I've seen love in many forms: the love of the game, the love between teammates, and the love that drives players to surpass their limits.

Love, in its purest form, is the ultimate motivator. It's not just about affection or attachment; it's about a deep, driving force that propels us forward, even in the face of adversity. On the basketball court, love is the energy that fuels those grueling practices, the long hours of training, and the relentless pursuit of excellence. It's the glue that binds a team together, transforming a group of individuals into a unified force.

But love's influence extends beyond the boundaries of the court. In my own life, love has been the anchor that has kept me grounded and the sail that has propelled me forward. As a young black man navigating the complexities of life and career, love for my community, my heritage, and my purpose has guided my decisions and shaped my path.

One of the most profound lessons I've learned about love is its ability to inspire growth and change. I remember a player who struggled with self-doubt and a lack of confidence. It was love - not just our belief in her, but her growing love for herself and her abilities - that turned the tide. As she learned to love and appreciate her own talents, her performance transformed. This wasn't a change born out of fear of failure or desire for accolades; it was a change inspired by love.

Love also has the power to heal and unite. In times of conflict or uncertainty within the team, it's the underlying love for each other and the game that brings us back together, realigning our focus and strengthening our bonds. Love fosters empathy, understanding, and cooperation, turning challenges into opportunities for strengthening relationships.

Moreover, love in coaching goes beyond the technical aspects of the game. It's about genuinely caring for the players, understanding their journeys, their struggles, and their aspirations. This form of love builds trust and respect, creating an environment where players feel valued and empowered. It's about nurturing not just athletes but individuals, guiding them in their growth both on and off the court.

As you read this chapter, consider the role of love in your own life. How has love driven you, shaped you, and transformed you? Love is not just a passive feeling; it's an active force that can guide your choices, fuel your passions, and lead you to your highest potential.

In conclusion, love is the ultimate driving force in our lives. It's a power that goes beyond emotion, influencing our beliefs, our actions, and our destiny. Whether it's the love of a sport, a passion, a person, or a cause, it's this love that drives us to achieve, to overcome, and to grow. As we navigate the complexities of life, let love be the force that guides us, propels us, and ultimately, transforms us.

Love as a Motivator: The Heartbeat of Our Journey

Love is a cornerstone of motivation. It's a force far greater than any external reward or recognition. Love, in its various forms, serves as a compass that directs us toward kindness, compassion, and connection. It's the heartbeat of our journey, both in sports and in life.

Love as a motivator manifests in myriad ways. On the basketball court, it's the love for the game that drives players to push their limits, to wake up before dawn for practice, and to keep going when their bodies scream for rest. It's a love that goes beyond personal glory; it's about being part of something greater, about honoring the game and those who played it before us.

But the scope of love's motivation extends beyond the bounds of athletic endeavor. In my personal life, love has been the driving force behind major decisions and daily actions. It's love for my family that has guided me through tough times, providing strength when I needed it most. It's love for my community that has driven me to be more than just a coach, but a mentor and a role model for young people who are navigating their own complex paths.

Love motivates us to act with kindness and compassion. In a world often driven by competition and individual success, love reminds us of the importance of connection and empathy. It's the force that compels us to help a struggling teammate, to listen when someone needs to talk, and to offer support when it's not asked for. This kind of motivation is not about personal gain; it's about building something bigger than ourselves.

Furthermore, love fuels our desire for connection. In the teams I've coached, the strongest bonds were not formed over victories, but over shared love for the game and for each other. This connection transcends the court, creating relationships that last a lifetime. It's a powerful reminder that our greatest achievements in life are not trophies or titles, but the connections we make and the lives we touch.

As you reflect on your own experiences, think about how love has motivated you. How has it driven you to act, to change, and to grow? Love is not a passive feeling that happens to us; it's an active force that we can choose to cultivate and follow. It's a source of strength, guiding us towards actions that are rooted in compassion and connection.

I want to emphasize that love is the ultimate driving force in our lives. It propels us forward, not just towards our goals, but towards becoming better versions of ourselves. Whether it's the love for a sport, a passion, a person, or a collective cause, it's this love that empowers us to achieve, to overcome challenges, and to grow beyond our imagined limits. In the complexities and challenges of life, let love be the force that guides your way, propelling you towards a life of fulfillment and transformation.

The Healing Power of Love: Mending Hearts and Bridging Divides

I have come to witness the profound healing power of love. It's a force that not only drives us but also has the remarkable ability to mend emotional wounds, bridge divides, and foster understanding and reconciliation. Love, in its essence, is a powerful healer, a balm that soothes the soul and mends the heart.

I've seen players come into the team carrying the weight of personal struggles and emotional scars. The court, for many, became a refuge, a place where the love for the game and the support of teammates provided a healing touch. This healing didn't erase their struggles, but it gave them the strength to face them. It was love that allowed them to open up, share their stories, and find comfort in the understanding and empathy of others.

One particular instance stands out in my memory. A player, who had experienced significant personal loss, was struggling to cope with the grief. The change in her was palpable - her performance declined, and her usual vibrant spirit dimmed. It was the collective love and support of the team that slowly helped her heal. We didn't just offer sympathy; we provided a space where she could grieve, heal, and eventually find her strength again. This healing process was a testament to the power of love in creating an environment where vulnerability is met with compassion and understanding.

Love also has the power to bridge divides, whether they are based on differences in background, beliefs, or experiences. In the diverse fabric of a team, it's love for each other and the game that unites us. This unity isn't about ignoring our differences but about embracing them, learning from them, and growing together. Love fosters a sense of belonging, where each member feels valued and understood.

Moreover, love plays a crucial role in reconciliation. In moments of conflict or misunderstanding within the team, it's the underlying love that brings us back to the table, ready to listen, understand, and reconcile. This process isn't always easy, but love provides the foundation for open dialogue and resolution. It reminds us that our shared goals and affections are greater than any conflict.

In your own life, think about the moments when love has healed you or helped you overcome a divide. Consider the times when love has brought about understanding and reconciliation in your relationships. Love is more than just a feeling - it's an action, a choice to embrace empathy, to offer support, and to seek understanding.

The healing power of love is a cornerstone of human experience. It has the ability to mend emotional wounds, bridge gaps of understanding, and bring about reconciliation. As we move through life, let's harness this power of love - in our families, our communities, and our teams. Let love be the force that heals, unites, and transforms us, guiding us towards a more compassionate and connected existence.

Love's Role in Decision-Making: Steering the Course of Our Lives

In the medley of life, love's influence on decision-making is both profound and far-reaching. Throughout my career and personal journey, I've observed and experienced how love shapes the courses we choose, guiding us toward paths that resonate with our deepest values and aspirations. Love, in its many dimensions, acts not just as an emotion, but as a compass directing our choices and actions.

In the realm of coaching, the decision to pursue this career was deeply rooted in love - love for the sport, love for teaching, and a profound love for impacting young lives. This wasn't a choice made from ambition alone; it was a calling fueled by passion and a deep desire to give back to the game that gave me so much. Love for basketball wasn't just about the game itself, but about the life lessons it imparts and the joy it brings to both players and spectators.

Similarly, the decisions made within the team, from strategies on the court to how we interact off it, are often influenced by the love we share for the sport and for each other. It's this love that drives us to work harder, to support one another, and to strive for excellence not just as individuals, but as a cohesive unit. Love binds the team together, creating a synergy where the whole becomes greater than the sum of its parts.

On a personal front, love has been a decisive factor in many of my life choices. From the relationships I've nurtured to the community initiatives I've participated in, love has been the guiding force. It's love that inspires me to be a better person, to extend a helping hand, and to make sacrifices for the greater good. These decisions, influenced by love, have not only brought fulfillment but have also shaped my character and life's trajectory.

Moreover, love's role in decision-making extends to how we respond to challenges and adversities. In moments of doubt or crisis, it's often the love for what we do, the people we care about, and our core beliefs that guides us through. Love provides clarity in confusion and strength in weakness, enabling us to make choices that align with our true selves.

As you navigate through your own life, reflect on how love has influenced your decisions. How has it shaped your career path, your relationships, and your view of the world? Recognize that love, in all its forms, is a powerful decision-making tool. It's not about choosing what's easy or convenient, but what resonates with your deepest values and aspirations.

I urge you to consider love as a critical lens through which to view your choices. Love, in its essence, is about connection - to people, to passions, to purposes. Let it guide you in your decisions, big and small. For in the end, it's love that gives meaning to our choices, love that enriches our journey, and love that ultimately defines who we are and what we become.

The Heart of the Game: Love as Life's Guiding Force

I have come to understand and appreciate love as the most potent and transformative force in our lives. It's a power that transcends mere emotion, actively shaping our actions, beliefs, and destinies. As a coach, I've been privileged to witness love in its many forms: the love of the game, the love among teammates, and the deep, personal love that pushes us to exceed our own expectations.

Love, in its truest form, emerges as the ultimate motivator. It's not confined to mere affection or attachment; it's a deep-seated force that propels us forward against all odds. On the basketball court, love is the fuel for grueling practices, intense training sessions, and the pursuit of excellence. It binds a team together, turning a collection of individuals into a single, unified entity driven by a shared passion.

Beyond the court, love has been my anchor and sail, guiding me through the complexities of life. As a young Black man forging a path in a world filled with challenges, love for my community, heritage, and purpose has been a guiding light, influencing my decisions and shaping my journey.

One lesson that stands out in my coaching career is love's power to inspire growth and transformation. I recall a player who struggled with self-doubt and lacked confidence. It wasn't just our belief in her abilities but her burgeoning love for herself and her skills that catalyzed a remarkable change. This transformation was not motivated by fear of failure or a hunger for accolades but was a manifestation of love.

In times of team conflicts or uncertainties, love has been the healing force that reunites and realigns. It fosters empathy, understanding, and cooperation, turning potential discord into opportunities for strengthening bonds. This aspect of love in coaching transcends the technicalities of the game, encompassing a genuine concern for players' journeys, struggles, and aspirations. It's about building trust and respect, creating an environment where players feel empowered and valued, not just as athletes but as individuals.

Reflecting on your own life, consider how love has driven, shaped, and transformed you. Love is not a mere passive feeling; it's an active force that guides your choices, fuels your passions, and elevates you to your highest potential.

In conclusion, love stands as the ultimate driving force in our lives. It's an energy that surpasses emotion, influencing our beliefs, actions, and fate. Whether it's love for a sport, a passion, a person, or a cause, it's this love that propels us to achieve, overcome, and grow. As we navigate life's complexities, let love be the force that guides, propels, and ultimately transforms us.

Love, as a motivator, is the heartbeat of our journey. It's more powerful than any external reward, serving as a compass towards kindness, compassion, and connection. This motivator manifests in various ways, from the love for the game that drives players to their limits to the love that unites teams and creates lasting bonds.

Lastly, love's role in decision-making cannot be overstated. It's a lens through which we view our choices, guiding us toward paths that resonate with our deepest values. Love influences our career paths, relationships, and worldviews, proving itself as a critical tool in our decision-making process.

In this chapter, I invite you to view love not just as an emotion but as life's guiding force, steering you through decisions, challenges, and towards a fulfilling journey. For, in the end, it is love that defines who we are and what we become.

The Symphony of Existence: Belief, Fear, and Love

Chapter 3

I have come to understand that the interplay of belief, fear, and love shapes not just the paths we tread but the very essence of our being. As a coach and a mentor, my journey has been illuminated by these three powerful forces, each playing a crucial role in the symphony of existence.

Belief is the spark that ignites the flame of potential. In my early days of coaching, I witnessed how a strong belief in oneself could turn the tide of a game, transforming doubt into confidence, fear into focus. Belief acts as a lens through which we view the world and ourselves, coloring our perceptions and decisions. It is the foundation upon which we build our dreams and aspirations.

Yet, alongside belief, there lurks fear, an ever-present shadow. Fear, in its essence, is a paradox - both a protector and an inhibitor. It has the power to paralyze, to cloud judgment, and to prevent us from seizing opportunities. But it also serves as a cautionary tale, a guide that reminds us of our vulnerabilities and the need for preparedness. In my coaching career, navigating fear has been as much about understanding its roots as it is about fostering courage and resilience in the face of it.

Amidst belief and fear, love emerges as the ultimate driving force. It is the energy that fuels passion, the bond that unites teams, and the healing balm that mends wounds. Love transcends the confines of mere emotion, becoming a catalyst for growth, change, and unity. In the teams I've coached, it's the love for the game, for each other, and for the journey that has often been the difference between victory and defeat.

The interplay of these forces is a delicate balance, a dance that requires both grace and strength. Belief without love can become arrogance, fear without belief can lead to paralysis, and love without the grounding of belief and the awareness of fear can be blind. The key lies in harmonizing these elements, in understanding their individual roles, and in leveraging their collective power.

As a coach, my role has often been to orchestrate this symphony - to instill belief in the hearts of my players, to help them navigate their fears, and to foster a culture of love and respect. It's about creating an environment where these forces can coexist and complement each other, leading to not just success on the court but growth and fulfillment in life.

As you reflect on your own journey, consider how belief, fear, and love have shaped your path. How have these forces interacted in your life? Have they been in harmony, or have they clashed? Understanding this interplay is crucial to navigating life's complexities.

The dance of belief, fear, and love is a continuous one, a symphony that plays out in every aspect of our lives. It's about striking a balance, understanding the role each plays, and utilizing their combined strength to propel us forward. As we move through life's journey, let us embrace this symphony, allowing it to guide us, shape us, and lead us to our true potential.

The Balancing Act: Navigating the Dynamics of Belief, Fear, and Love

This trio of forces operates like a delicate balancing act, each one influencing and being influenced by the others. Their interplay is complex, and understanding it has been crucial in both guiding my players and navigating my own life decisions.

Belief, as the starting point, sets the stage for what we think is possible. It's the driving force that propels us forward, igniting the fire of ambition and aspiration. However, belief, when untempered, can lead us astray. That's where fear steps in, serving as a balancing force. Fear, often perceived negatively, plays a critical role in keeping our feet grounded. It instills a sense of caution, urging us to consider the risks and consequences of our actions. This interplay between belief and fear is essential, ensuring that our decisions are both daring and prudent.

Then there's love, the force that infuses our actions with meaning and purpose. Love balances both belief and fear by providing a deeper reason for our pursuits. It's the glue that holds everything together, turning ambitions into passions and challenges into opportunities. In the context of coaching, it's love for the game and the team that often becomes the deciding factor in how belief and fear are managed. Love inspires players to push past their fears, and it tempers their beliefs with empathy and collaboration.

Each of these forces - belief, fear, and love - does not operate in isolation. They are interconnected, each one influencing the intensity and direction of the others. Too much fear can stifle belief, while unchecked belief can lead to reckless decisions. Love, without the grounding of belief and the caution of fear, can become aimless. The art lies in balancing these elements, understanding their nuances, and using their combined power to navigate the complexities of life.

In practice, this balancing act plays out in every decision, every game plan, and every interaction. It's about encouraging players to believe in their abilities, while also preparing them to face and manage their fears. It's about fostering a team culture where love for the game and each other drives excellence, but not at the cost of personal well-being or team harmony.

For anyone navigating their path, understanding this dynamic is key. Reflect on your life decisions and the roles played by belief, fear, and love. How have they shaped your choices? Were they in balance, or did one dominate the others? Recognizing their interplay gives you a framework to make more informed, holistic decisions.

Personal Growth through Understanding: The Interplay of Belief, Fear, and Love

Delving deeper into my experiences as a coach and an individual, I have realized the profound personal growth and self-awareness that comes from understanding the roles of belief, fear, and love in shaping our lives. This trio of forces is not just about external manifestations; they are deeply intertwined with our inner growth and development.

Belief has been the cornerstone of my journey. It shaped my early dreams and laid the foundation for my career. But as I progressed, I recognized that unchecked belief could lead to overconfidence. The personal growth here was in learning to temper belief with humility and self-reflection. Understanding that belief is not static, but a dynamic force that needs nurturing and sometimes, recalibration, was pivotal. It led to a deeper self-awareness, where my strengths and limitations were equally acknowledged.

Fear, often a challenging companion, has been a significant catalyst for growth. Initially, it was an obstacle, something to overcome. However, with time and experience, I've learned that fear also serves as a teacher. It highlights areas where growth is needed, pushing me out of my comfort zone. Embracing fear, understanding its roots, and using it as a stepping stone rather than a stumbling block has been transformative. This process has fostered a level of self-awareness that goes beyond mere acknowledgment of fear. It's about engaging with it, learning from it, and allowing it to shape me in ways that foster resilience and courage.

Love, in its multifaceted nature, has been the most profound in terms of personal growth. It has taught me empathy, patience, and the true meaning of strength. In coaching, love for my players meant wanting the best for them, which often required tough decisions and hard conversations. It also meant learning to balance the drive for success with the wellbeing of the team. This understanding of love has extended to my personal life, teaching me the value of deep connections, the strength in vulnerability, and the power of genuine care. It's a continuous journey of understanding the depths of love and its impact on both personal and interpersonal dynamics.

The interplay of these forces - belief, fear, and love - is a complex dance that shapes our decisions, our interactions, and our path in life. In my journey, this understanding has led to a heightened level of self-awareness. It has allowed me to navigate life with a clearer sense of purpose, understanding, and compassion. The balance between these forces is never perfect, and the learning never stops. Each day brings new insights, new challenges, and new opportunities for growth.

Understanding the roles of belief, fear, and love in our lives is a journey of continuous personal growth and self-discovery. It's about recognizing how these forces shape us and using that knowledge to navigate life with greater awareness and purpose. As we embrace this journey, we find ourselves evolving, not just as professionals, coaches, or leaders, but as individuals - richer in experience, wisdom, and empathy. Let this symphony of existence guide you, challenge you, and inspire you to reach your fullest potential.

Case Studies: Life Lessons from the Court to the Heart

These case studies, drawn from my coaching experience and personal observations, illustrate how understanding these elements can lead to significant life changes.

1. **The Underdog's Triumph**: One of my most memorable experiences involved a player I'll call Sarah. Sarah joined the team with raw talent but lacked self-belief. She was constantly shadowed by fear - fear of failure, of not being good enough. It was through fostering a culture of love and support within the team that we began to see a transformation. As her teammates and I showed unwavering belief in her abilities, Sarah started to overcome her fears. By the end of the season, she had become one of our star players, not because her skills had

drastically changed, but because her belief in herself had. This case underscored the power of belief and love in conquering fear and unlocking potential.

2. **The Veteran's Dilemma**: Another case involved a seasoned player, Mark, who was contemplating retirement due to a waning passion for the game. He was torn between the fear of the unknown outside basketball and the comfort of the familiar. Through conversations that centered around love - love for the game, for personal growth, and for life beyond the court - Mark found clarity. He realized that his fear was holding him back from exploring new avenues where he could apply his leadership and teamwork skills. His decision to retire and pursue a career in youth mentoring was a

testament to the role of love in guiding life-changing decisions, balancing the fear of change with the belief in new beginnings.

3. **The Coach's Challenge**: My personal journey has not been immune to these dynamics. Early in my career, I faced significant challenges that tested my belief in my coaching abilities. The fear of not living up to expectations was overwhelming. However, it was the love for the game and my genuine desire to impact young lives that kept me anchored. This love allowed me to push through the fear and bolster my belief in my methods and philosophy. The experience taught me that love could be a powerful motivator, enabling us to face fears and reinforce our beliefs.

These stories from the court reflect broader life lessons. They demonstrate how belief, fear, and love are not isolated forces but are deeply interconnected, each playing a vital role in our growth and decision-making processes. They show that understanding and balancing these elements can lead to profound personal and professional transformations.

As we journey through life, it is crucial to recognize the roles played by belief, fear, and love. Their interplay is a constant dance, one that requires awareness and skill to navigate. These case studies are a testament to the power of understanding these dynamics. They serve as reminders that, regardless of our roles - be it as athletes, coaches, professionals, or simply as individuals navigating the complexities of life - the synergy of belief, fear, and love is fundamental to our growth and fulfillment. Let these stories inspire you to embrace and balance these forces in your life, leading to a journey marked by resilience, compassion, and purposeful living.

The Harmony of Human Essence: Belief, Fear, and Love

Belief has been my compass, directing me through both triumphs and tribulations. It's the force that lights the spark of potential and keeps the flame of hope burning, even in the darkest of times. But belief, in its absolute form, can lead us astray. Herein lies the significance of fear - not as an enemy, but as a cautious friend. Fear reminds us of our limits, nudges us to prepare, and often saves us from the perils of overconfidence. It keeps our beliefs grounded in reality.

Yet, the most powerful of all these forces is love. Love, in its unbounded grace, is the catalyst that transforms potential into reality, fear into courage, and individuals into communities. It's the force that unites, heals, and propels us towards our highest aspirations. In my coaching journey, it has been love - for the game, for my players, for the shared journey - that has made the most significant impact. It is love that turns a group of individuals into a team, a game into a life lesson, and a coach into a mentor.

This symphony of belief, fear, and love plays an endless melody, a harmony that resonates through every aspect of our lives. It's a delicate balance, a dance that requires awareness, understanding, and sometimes, a leap of faith. As we navigate through the complexities of life, let us be mindful of this interplay. Let us embrace the lessons that each of these forces brings, and let us find our rhythm in their melody.

To conclude this chapter, I extend an invitation to you, the reader, to reflect on your own journey. How have belief, fear, and love shaped your path? Have they been in harmony, or have they clashed? Understanding this dynamic is not just an exercise in introspection; it is a step towards deeper self-awareness, towards a life lived with purpose and understanding.

As we turn the pages of our lives, let us cherish this symphony of existence. Let it guide us, challenge us, and inspire us. In the grand scheme of things, it is belief, fear, and love that make us truly human, that shape our dreams, guide our journeys, and define our legacies. Let this harmony lead you to a life of fulfillment, growth, and profound meaning.

The Essence of Belief: The Core of Our Existence

Chapter 4

Belief is much more than a mental state. It's an active force that propels us forward, a beacon that guides us through the fog of uncertainty. In my years on the basketball court, I've seen belief act as the wind beneath the wings of players, lifting them to heights they never imagined possible. It's the force that turns dreams into goals, and goals into achievements. When a player truly believes in their ability, their potential becomes limitless.

But belief's power extends beyond the physical realms of a basketball game. It's a foundational element of our very being. In the communities I've worked with, belief has been a cornerstone - belief in a better future, belief in the power of unity, and belief in the inherent strength of our shared humanity. This kind of belief ignites a fire of change, a fire that can spread and transform entire communities.

Belief, however, is not a standalone entity. It exists in a dynamic interplay with fear and love, as I've discussed in previous chapters. While fear can challenge belief, acting as a counterforce that tests its strength, love can amplify and solidify it. The relationship between these elements is intricate and profound. Love nurtures belief, giving it depth and resilience, while belief can conquer fear, turning obstacles into stepping stones.

As a coach, I've often seen belief act as a life force in moments of adversity. When the odds were stacked against us, when the whispers of doubt grew louder, it was belief that kept us anchored. It was the belief in our collective strength, in the power of our shared vision, and in the unwavering support we had for each other, that saw us through. This kind of belief transcends the physical aspects of the game; it touches the soul and ignites a passion that is infectious.

The nature of belief as a life force is also evident in personal growth and self-awareness. When we believe in ourselves, in our capabilities, and in our worth, we open doors to infinite possibilities. This belief is not about arrogance or blind optimism; it's a grounded understanding of our potential and our power to effect change, both in ourselves and in the world around us.

In my own life, belief has been the driving force behind every decision, every challenge, and every victory. It has been the light that guided me through dark times and the strength that carried me over hurdles. This belief, rooted in love and tempered by an understanding of fear, has been my greatest ally.

As you turn the pages of this book, and as you navigate the chapters of your life, I encourage you to reflect on the nature of your beliefs. What do you believe about yourself, your abilities, and your place in the world? How does your belief interact with your fears and your love? Remember, belief is not just a thought; it's a life force, a catalyst that shapes your journey. Harness this force, let it guide you, and watch as it transforms your world.

Belief, in its essence, is the genesis of all we dare to dream and all we dare to achieve. Let it be your companion, your guide, and your strength as you journey through the complexities of life. Embrace the power of belief, and let it be the force that propels you towards your highest potential, in basketball and beyond.

Understanding Belief in Relation to Scientific Theories

Belief, as I have come to understand, is not just a personal or spiritual concept; it is also fundamentally intertwined with the realms of scientific inquiry and theories. This connection between belief and science might seem paradoxical at first, especially when one considers the empirical nature of scientific methods. However, belief is at the core of scientific progress, serving as the bedrock upon which hypotheses are built and new frontiers are explored.

At its core, belief in science is about embracing possibilities and venturing into the unknown. Every scientific inquiry begins with a belief - a belief in a hypothesis, in the potential of an experiment, or in the existence of an unseen phenomenon. This belief is what drives scientists to ask questions, to challenge existing paradigms, and to push the boundaries of knowledge. Without this initial leap of faith, the scientific method cannot begin. It is belief that fuels the curiosity and determination to seek answers, to test and retest, and to eventually arrive at conclusions that can withstand rigorous scrutiny.

The impact of belief systems on scientific advancements cannot be overstated. History is replete with examples of scientists who, driven by their belief in the potential of their work, have revolutionized our understanding of the world. From Galileo's belief in a heliocentric solar system to Einstein's belief in the relativity of space and time, it's clear that belief is a catalyst for scientific breakthroughs. These beliefs, often in the face of skepticism and opposition, have paved the way for discoveries that have shaped modern science.

However, the intersection of faith and empirical evidence in science is a delicate balance. Science requires evidence, rigor, and the ability to question and disprove. Yet, it also necessitates a belief in the unseen and unproven, at least initially. This balance is crucial; too much skepticism can hinder innovation, while blind faith can lead to pseudoscience. The greatest scientific minds have mastered this balance, using belief as a compass to guide their inquiry, while relying on empirical evidence to validate or refute their theories.

In my coaching career, I've seen parallels in how belief intersects with the strategies and techniques we employ. Just as scientists believe in their hypotheses, coaches believe in their game plans, training methods, and the potential of their players. This belief, backed by experience and observation, guides our decisions and strategies. However, just like in science, we must be willing to adapt and change our beliefs when faced with new evidence or outcomes.

As we delve deeper into the chapters of this book and our lives, it's essential to appreciate the role of belief in both scientific and personal realms. Understanding belief in relation to scientific theories offers a profound perspective on how we perceive and interact with the world. It encourages us to question, explore, and constantly seek truth, guided by a balanced interplay of belief and empirical evidence.

The Role of Belief in Life's Direction

Belief profoundly influences the direction of our lives, shaping our choices, paths, and ultimately, our destinies. As I reflect on my journey, both on and off the basketball court, I recognize how personal beliefs, cultivated through experiences and interactions, have steered my decisions and actions. These beliefs, deeply ingrained, often act as silent architects, constructing the narrative of our lives.

In the realm of coaching, my belief in the potential of every player, regardless of their background or initial skill level, has driven my approach. This belief has led me to invest time and energy in developing each player, often leading to transformative outcomes. It's not just about honing their skills in the game but about instilling a belief in their own capabilities, which extends beyond the court into their personal lives.

The influence of cultural and societal beliefs on individual decisions is significant. Growing up as a young black man, the societal beliefs and stereotypes about race and capability inevitably impacted me. However, it was the belief instilled in me by my mentors - a belief in equality, perseverance, and the power of hard work - that shaped my path. This underscores the impact of the larger belief systems we are part of and how they can either limit or empower us.

The transformative power of changing beliefs is perhaps the most striking. Throughout my career, I've witnessed players and colleagues who, when they altered their beliefs, experienced profound changes in their lives. A player who once believed she wasn't leadership material, upon changing that belief, transformed into an inspiring team captain. This shift in belief can open up new possibilities, allowing us to reimagine and reshape our futures.

As a coach, I have also had to reassess and change my beliefs. What worked in one era of coaching did not necessarily apply in another. Adapting my beliefs about strategies, team dynamics, and even leadership styles was essential for growth and relevance. This flexibility in beliefs is crucial, not just in sports but in all facets of life.

In understanding the role of belief in life's direction, it's important to recognize that our beliefs are not fixed. They are fluid, evolving with new experiences, knowledge, and understanding. Embracing this dynamism in beliefs allows us to remain open to growth, to challenge our limitations, and to embrace change.

The journey of life is, in many ways, a journey of belief - from the beliefs we inherit to the ones we adopt and eventually, the ones we pass on. As you navigate through the chapters of this book and your life, reflect on the beliefs that have shaped your path. Consider how they have influenced your decisions, your relationships, and your sense of self. Be open to examining and redefining these beliefs, for in doing so, you unlock the potential for transformation and empowerment.

Belief, in its essence, is a powerful life force - a force that can either confine us to the familiar or propel us into the realms of the extraordinary. Embrace it with awareness and intention, and let it guide you towards a life of fulfillment and purpose.

Personal Reflection: Yesterday's Beliefs vs. Today's Realities

Reflecting on my own life, I realize how the evolution of beliefs over time has shaped who I am today. As a young man, my beliefs were shaped by my environment, my family, and the cultural narratives of the time. I believed in hard work, resilience, and the power of a dream. These beliefs were instrumental in pushing me towards my goals, in coaching and beyond.

However, as I journeyed through life, I encountered experiences and information that challenged these early beliefs. I learned that hard work, while essential, wasn't always enough; systemic barriers and inequalities played a significant role in shaping outcomes. My belief in the power of a dream evolved to include the need for awareness, advocacy, and action in addressing these broader societal issues.

This process of adapting beliefs in the face of new information and experiences is a testament to personal growth. It's about being open to learning, to questioning, and to changing. In my coaching career, adapting my beliefs meant evolving my strategies to fit the changing dynamics of the game and the diverse needs of my players. It involved embracing new techniques, new technologies, and, most importantly, new perspectives on leadership and teamwork.

The impact of past beliefs on current realities is profound. My early belief in the importance of discipline and hard work laid the foundation for my career. However, it was the evolution of these beliefs - the incorporation of empathy, understanding, and adaptability - that truly defined my success and impact as a coach.

The transformative power of changing beliefs is one of life's most potent forces. It allows us to grow, to evolve, and to better align our inner values with the outer world. In my case, the belief in the transformative power of sports remained constant, but how I approached and implemented this belief changed significantly over time.

In conclusion, understanding the interplay between yesterday's beliefs and today's realities is crucial in navigating life's journey. It involves a continuous process of learning, unlearning, and relearning. As you read this book and reflect on your own journey, I encourage you to consider how your beliefs have evolved and how they have shaped your current reality. Embrace the process of adapting your beliefs, for it is through this evolution that we grow, learn, and truly come into our own.

Belief, in all its forms, is the bedrock upon which we build our lives. Let your beliefs be dynamic, informed by experience and wisdom, and let them guide you towards a life of fulfillment, purpose, and continuous growth.

The Dynamics of Self in Time and Space

Chapter 5

As I stand today, reflecting on the journey that has led me here, I am struck by the profound interplay of time, space, and self-perception in shaping our lives. In the realm of basketball coaching, this interplay manifests in unique ways, illuminating broader truths about our existence and our perception of self.

Time, in my experience, is a relentless teacher. It has taught me patience, resilience, and the value of perspective. As a young coach, time seemed infinite, and success felt like it should come swiftly. However, as years passed, I learned that true success, both on and off the court, is a product of time - time spent practicing, learning, failing, and growing. Time has a way of refining our skills, honing our beliefs, and shaping our visions. It's in the crucible of time that our true selves are forged.

Space, or the environments we inhabit, also plays a critical role in our self-perception. The basketball court, for me, was more than just a physical space; it was a realm of possibility, a place where belief, fear, and love converged to create something magical. This space shaped my identity as a coach and as an individual. It was here that I learned the power of teamwork, the importance of strategy, and the beauty of collective effort. However, it's not just the physical spaces that matter; it's the communities, the cultures, and the societal contexts that surround us. These spaces influence our beliefs, our fears, and our capacity for love, molding our perceptions of ourselves and our potential.

Self-perception is perhaps the most intriguing aspect of this triad. How we see ourselves determines not just our actions, but also the paths we choose to walk. As a coach, my self-perception evolved dramatically over the years. I began as someone who saw coaching primarily as a means to win games. However, over time, I came to see myself as a mentor, a leader, and a catalyst for positive change in the lives of my players. This shift in self-perception wasn't abrupt; it was a gradual process influenced by time, experiences, and the spaces I inhabited.

The interplay of time, space, and self-perception is a dynamic dance, constantly in motion, shaping and reshaping our identities and our destinies. In my coaching career, this interplay manifested in how I approached each season, each game, and each player. It influenced my strategies, my communication, and my understanding of my role as a coach.

In the wider context of life, this interplay is equally significant. Our perception of time influences our urgency, our patience, and our approach to life's challenges. The spaces we occupy - be it our homes, workplaces, or communities - shape our views, our interactions, and our sense of self. And our self-perception dictates how we engage with the world, how we tackle obstacles, and how we pursue our goals.

As we delve deeper into this chapter, and as you reflect on your own journey, consider how time, space, and self-perception have played a role in shaping who you are. How has your perception of time influenced your decisions? In what ways have the spaces you've inhabited shaped your beliefs and actions? And how has your self-perception evolved over the years?

Remember, the dynamics of self in time and space are not fixed; they are fluid, ever-changing, and responsive to our experiences and choices. Embrace this fluidity, for it is in this dance of time, space, and self-perception that we find the essence of growth, the beauty of transformation, and the true path to realizing our potential.

How Belief and Choice Remake Time and Space

Time and space, in their conventional sense, are constants. However, our perception of them is anything but. It's fluid, shaped by our beliefs, choices, and experiences. The concept that time can seem to fly or drag depending on our state of mind is not just a psychological phenomenon;

it's a testament to the power of our beliefs and choices in shaping our reality.

Take, for instance, the final minutes of a closely contested basketball game. For the players on the court, those minutes can feel like an eternity, each second laden with the weight of potential victory or defeat. For the spectators, time might seem to fly, as they are caught up in the excitement of the game. This subjective experience of time is influenced by our engagement, our emotions, and our anticipation - all products of our belief and choices.

Similarly, space is perceived differently based on our beliefs and the choices we make. A basketball court is more than just a physical area bounded by lines; it's a space where dreams are pursued, challenges are faced, and triumphs are celebrated. For a player who believes in their potential and chooses to embrace the challenge, the court becomes a space of opportunity. For another, clouded by doubt and fear, the same space can feel intimidating and restrictive.

The psychological implications of this concept are profound. They suggest that by altering our beliefs and choices, we can change our experience of reality. This understanding is empowering. It means that we have the power to change our perception of our circumstances, to transform challenges into opportunities, and to view our journey through a lens of growth and possibility.

Philosophically, this concept challenges us to reconsider the nature of reality itself. If our perception of time and space can be so deeply influenced by our internal states, then what is the true nature of these dimensions? This question invites us to explore the intersection of reality, perception, and consciousness.

There are numerous examples where belief has altered perceptions of time and space. In sports, athletes often speak of being 'in the zone' - a state where time seems to slow down, allowing them to perform with heightened focus and skill. This state is a product of belief in oneself and the choice to fully engage in the moment.

In life, too, our perception of time and space shifts with our beliefs and choices. Consider the difference in how time feels when we are doing something we love versus when we are engaged in a task we find tedious. The former can make hours feel like minutes, while the latter can make minutes feel like hours.

As you navigate through this chapter and your own life, reflect on how your beliefs and choices are shaping your perception of time and space. Consider how altering these beliefs and choices might change your experience of reality. Embrace the power you hold in shaping your world, and remember that the true essence of time and space lies not in their objective measurement, but in how we choose to perceive and experience them.

The Ongoing Influence from Birth to Death: Navigating Life's Journey

As a coach, my beliefs were rooted in ambition and a straightforward approach to success. But as I progressed, navigating through various challenges and triumphs, my beliefs evolved. I realized the complexity of human dynamics and the multifaceted nature of success. This evolution in belief was not just a change in thought; it was a transformation in how I perceived time and space, and ultimately, myself.

The role of evolving self-perception in shaping one's understanding of time and space is significant. Early in my career, time felt abundant, and space was merely a physical dimension. However, with experience, my perception shifted. Time became a valuable entity, not just in terms of minutes and hours but as moments of impact and change. Space transformed from mere physicality to an arena of emotional and psychological interactions.

Reflecting on the continuous interplay between belief and personal growth, it's evident that our beliefs are not static. They are shaped by our experiences, our interactions, and our introspections. A belief that once seemed unshakable may evolve or even dissolve with new insights and experiences. This fluidity in belief is essential for growth, allowing us to adapt and thrive in an ever-changing world.

In the context of coaching, the beliefs I instilled in my players went beyond the strategies of basketball. It was about instilling beliefs in their potential, their resilience, and their ability to overcome challenges. These beliefs, nurtured over time, influenced not only their performance on the court but also their approach to life. The players' evolving perceptions of themselves, influenced by their experiences and growth, shaped their journey, both as athletes and individuals.

The journey from birth to death is a tapestry woven with beliefs, choices, and perceptions. Each stage of life brings new challenges, experiences, and insights, influencing our belief system and reshaping our perception of the world. The beliefs we hold in childhood, the rebellious questioning of adolescence, the ambitious pursuits of young adulthood, and the reflective wisdom of maturity - each phase contributes to the mosaic of our existence.

In navigating this journey, it's crucial to remain open to the evolution of beliefs. Holding onto outdated beliefs can limit our potential and hinder our growth. The process of adapting beliefs in the face of new information and experiences is not a sign of inconsistency; it's a mark of wisdom and maturity. It's about being receptive to learning, unlearning, and relearning throughout life's journey.

In conclusion, the interplay of time, space, and self-perception, shaped by our evolving beliefs, is what defines our journey through life. As you reflect on your own path, consider how your beliefs have changed over time and how they have influenced your perception of yourself and the world. Embrace the continuous evolution of beliefs as a natural and essential part of personal growth. Let this understanding guide you through the diverse phases of life, helping you to navigate the complexities of existence with resilience, adaptability, and wisdom.

Quantum Trajectories: Life's Choices in Moments

The concept of life as a series of quantum choices is a compelling lens through which I have come to view my journey and the journeys of those I've coached. It's the idea that each decision we make, no matter how small, sets us on a path that shapes our trajectory, much like a quantum particle that exists in a multitude of states until a choice is made.

Reflecting on critical decisions in my life and career, I see how these moments have defined my path. From the decision to pursue coaching to the strategic choices made in crucial games, each has been a point of divergence, a quantum leap into a new set of possibilities. These decisions, influenced by my beliefs and experiences, have not only shaped my trajectory but also the lives of the players I've coached.

Beliefs play a pivotal role in these quantum moments. Our beliefs about ourselves, our abilities, and our potential influence the choices we make and the paths we take. In basketball, a player's belief in their capability to make a game-winning shot can be the difference between taking the shot or passing it up. Similarly, in life, our beliefs about what we can achieve and who we can become influence the decisions we make every day.

This concept has profound psychological and philosophical implications. It challenges us to consider the power of choice and the role of belief in shaping our reality. Every decision is a point of potential transformation, a moment where we can alter our path and redefine our destiny.

In my coaching, I've seen players face these quantum moments - times when their decisions on the court have altered the course of a game and, in some cases, their careers. These moments are microcosms of life's larger choices, where the interplay of belief, fear, and love comes into sharp focus. The decision to take a risk, to trust in one's abilities, or to make a sacrifice for the team - these are the moments that define us.

Moreover, the concept of quantum trajectories reminds us that life is not predestined but is shaped by a series of choices, each influenced by our beliefs and perceptions. It emphasizes the power we have to shape our journey and the importance of being conscious of the choices we make.

As we move through life, we encounter countless quantum moments - points where our decisions set us on new paths. Some of these decisions may seem insignificant at the time, but their cumulative effect can be profound. The choice to embrace a new opportunity, to change a long-held belief, or to take a stand on an issue - these are the moments that shape our trajectory and define who we are.

In conclusion, understanding life as a series of quantum choices offers a powerful perspective on the journey of self-discovery and growth. It highlights the significance of each decision we make and the role our beliefs play in shaping our path. As you navigate your own journey, consider the quantum moments you face and the trajectories they offer. Embrace the power of choice and belief, and let them guide you on a path of growth, transformation, and fulfillment.

The Sudden Impact of Love

Chapter 6

I have come to understand the sudden and profound impact of love. This force, often unexpected in its arrival, has the power to transform the very fabric of our lives. It's like a lightning bolt that illuminates our world in a way we never thought possible.

Love, in its essence, is an enigma. It appears in various forms and affects each of us differently. On the basketball court, I've witnessed the love of the game act as a catalyst, driving players to push beyond their perceived limits. The love between teammates fosters a bond that transcends the game itself, creating a unity that is palpable both on and off the court. This kind of love is not just about winning games; it's about building relationships and creating an environment where everyone feels valued and supported.

But the impact of love goes far beyond the boundaries of sports. In my personal life, love has been a guiding force, shaping my decisions and my path. It's a love for my family, my community, and the principles I stand for. This love has given me strength in times of adversity and clarity in moments of confusion. It's a reminder of what truly matters in life - the connections we make, the lives we touch, and the legacy we leave behind.

The sudden impact of love can be transformative. It can change our perspective, alter our priorities, and redefine our purpose. I remember a player who, despite her talent, struggled with self-confidence. It was the love and support of her teammates that eventually helped her realize her true potential. This love did not just change her performance on the court; it changed her perception of herself.

Love also has the power to heal. In my career, I've seen how love can mend the rifts within a team, bringing players back together after a conflict or a loss. It's a force that encourages empathy, fosters understanding, and promotes forgiveness. This healing aspect of love is essential, not only in sports but in all areas of life.

However, the sudden impact of love is not always easy. It challenges us to be vulnerable, to open ourselves up in ways that can be frightening. But it's in this vulnerability that we find true strength and connection. Love asks us to be our most authentic selves, to show up fully, and to engage with others in a meaningful way.

In conclusion, the sudden impact of love is a phenomenon that cannot be understated. It's a force that can change the course of a game, a life, a community. As you navigate through this chapter, and through your own life, be open to the impact of love. Let it guide you, transform you, and lead you to a deeper understanding of yourself and the world around you.

Reflecting on Fictional Love: The Influence of Characters on Our Lives

The impact of love, even when directed towards a fictional character, can be incredibly profound and transformational. This is exemplified in the way readers might find themselves enamored with a character like Louisa Rey from "Cloud Atlas." This fascination is not merely a passing admiration for a well-crafted character; it is a deep emotional connection that reflects the power of storytelling and its influence on our lives.

Falling in love with a character such as Louisa Rey is akin to encountering a soul that resonates with our deepest aspirations and fears. Her journey, marked by determination and resilience against overwhelming odds, mirrors the battles we face in our own lives. This connection transcends the pages of the novel and becomes a part of our emotional landscape.

The depth and intensity of this emotional experience are significant. It challenges our perceptions, alters our priorities, and can even redefine our purpose. Just as a coach observes a player's transformation through the love and support of their teammates, readers experience a similar transformation through their emotional investment in a character. This type of love can inspire us to seek similar qualities in our lives, motivate us to overcome our struggles, and provide a sense of comfort in moments of uncertainty.

Moreover, the influence of fictional characters like Louisa Rey extends beyond mere emotional stimulation; it shapes our beliefs and values. Characters become symbolic of ideals we strive for or fears we wish to conquer. They act as beacons, guiding us through the complexities of our emotions and beliefs, and often, they become a part of who we are.

The sudden impact of this kind of love reveals the capacity of the human heart to find connection and meaning in the most unexpected places. It demonstrates our ability to empathize and form bonds, even with entities that exist only in the realm of fiction. This phenomenon underscores the power of narrative and storytelling in shaping our understanding of ourselves and the world around us.

In conclusion, the sudden impact of love, whether for a person in our lives or a character in a story, is a testament to the boundless nature of our emotional capacity. It highlights the significant role that stories and characters play in our personal growth and understanding of human emotions. As we journey through life, these fictional loves remind us of the beauty and complexity of our inner worlds, and the endless possibilities of human connection and empathy.

The Possibility and Significance of Instantaneous Love

The idea of love striking suddenly, like a bolt of lightning, is often met with skepticism. However, in my experience, this form of love, though rare, is very real. It's a visceral response, a deep connection felt almost immediately upon encountering someone or something. On the basketball court, I've seen players fall in love with the game in an instant - a moment that defines their path for years to come. This immediate bond, though initially based on a surface-level attraction or connection, can grow into something deep, meaningful, and transformative.

The psychological mechanisms behind instantaneous love are complex. From a biological standpoint, it involves a cocktail of neurotransmitters and hormones that evoke feelings of excitement, happiness, and a strong bond. But beyond the biological explanation, there's a deeper emotional and spiritual aspect. Instantaneous love can be a recognition of something within the other that resonates deeply with our own inner selves. It's as if in that person, we see a reflection of our own aspirations, dreams, and unexpressed desires.

The significance and impact of this kind of love on an individual's life and beliefs are profound. It can change the course of a person's life, influencing decisions, shaping goals, and altering perceptions. In my own life, the love I felt for basketball the first time I stepped onto the court didn't just shape my career; it molded my values, my approach to relationships, and my understanding of teamwork and leadership.

However, this form of love is not without its challenges. It requires us to be open, vulnerable, and willing to explore the depths of our emotions. It asks us to trust our instincts and to believe in the potential of a connection that is yet to be fully understood. This can be daunting, but it is also where the beauty of this love lies - in its ability to open us up to new experiences, to teach us about trust and faith, and to propel us on a journey of self-discovery.

While the concept of love at first sight may be debated, its existence and impact are undeniable. Whether it's a love for a person, a passion, or a calling, its sudden impact can be a turning point in our lives. It challenges our beliefs, enriches our experiences, and adds a layer of depth and meaning to our existence. As we move forward in this chapter and in life, let us remain open to the possibilities of instantaneous love and the profound changes it can bring.

Embracing the Instant: The Power of Love at First Sight

In the panorama of human emotions, the idea of love at first sight stands as a beacon of intrigue and romanticism. My journey as a basketball coach has allowed me to witness the instantaneous connections that can form between people, ideas, and passions. The sudden, overwhelming sensation of love that strikes without warning - this is not just the stuff of poetry and novels; it's a profound human experience that deserves exploration and understanding.

The concept of love at first sight challenges our rational understanding of emotions. It's often dismissed as infatuation or a superficial attraction. Yet, in my experience, this instantaneous love can be a genuine recognition of a deep-seated connection. It's as if, in that moment of first encounter, there's a profound alignment of values, desires, and spirits. On the basketball court, I've seen players instantly fall in love with the game, a moment that becomes a defining turning point in their lives. This immediate bond may start with admiration but soon transforms into a deep, abiding love.

Analyzing the psychological and emotional mechanisms behind this phenomenon, we find a complex interplay of instinct, intuition, and subconscious desires. From a biological perspective, instantaneous love triggers a surge of neurotransmitters and hormones, creating a potent cocktail of emotions. But on a deeper level, this kind of love taps into our innate longing for connection, recognition, and understanding. It speaks to the part of us that seeks a mirror in another - be it a person, a passion, or a pursuit.

The significance of instantaneous love in shaping our lives and beliefs cannot be overstated. This form of love can redefine our priorities, alter our trajectories, and profoundly impact our worldview. In my own journey, the immediate love I felt for coaching reshaped my entire life. It influenced my career choices, my relationships, and my approach to challenges. This instant connection was not just about the thrill of the game; it was a recognition of my purpose and calling.

However, embracing instantaneous love requires a willingness to be vulnerable, to trust the authenticity of our feelings, and to be open to the transformation it brings. It's a leap of faith, a surrender to the unknown. This form of love asks us to trust our instincts, to embrace the moment, and to allow ourselves to be swept away by the current of deep emotional connection.

The possibility and significance of instantaneous love, or love at first sight, are profound. It's a testament to the depth and complexity of human emotions. As we navigate the chapters of this book and our lives, let us be open to the power of instant connections. Let us embrace the possibility of finding love in a single moment, for it's in these moments that our lives can be irrevocably changed. The sudden impact of love is not just a fanciful notion; it's a reality that can bring depth, joy, and meaning to our existence.

Exploring the Depth of Newly Formed Emotional Bonds

The depth and complexities of emotions in newly formed relationships are remarkable. These relationships, whether between a coach and a player or among teammates, begin with initial impressions and beliefs. These first encounters set the tone for the bond that follows. In my coaching experience, I have seen how a player's belief in their potential, or lack thereof, can shape the initial dynamics of our relationship. A belief in their capabilities, coupled with mutual respect and understanding, often lays the groundwork for a strong, enduring bond.

These early emotional connections are not just fleeting moments; they have the potential for long-term impact. The support, trust, and camaraderie developed in the early stages of a coach-player relationship can influence a player's entire career. The belief instilled in them, the love for the game nurtured, and the fear of failure conquered - these elements intertwine to shape not only their athletic journey but also their life beyond the court.

The role of initial impressions and beliefs in forming these bonds is pivotal. As a coach, the belief I hold about a player's potential from our first interaction can significantly influence our relationship's trajectory. If I believe in their potential, it can foster a bond of trust and encouragement, propelling them to greater heights. Conversely, a lack of belief can hinder the bond and, consequently, the player's growth.

In the realm of basketball, as in life, the emotional bonds we form are often reflections of our deepest beliefs and fears. A coach's belief in a player's potential, a player's love for the game, and the collective fear of not reaching their goals - these emotions create a tapestry of relationships that are both complex and profound.

Reflecting on the long-term impact of these early emotional connections, it becomes clear that they shape more than just athletic performance. They influence character development, resilience, teamwork, and the ability to face challenges both on and off the court. The bond formed between a coach and a player, or among teammates, often becomes a microcosm of the larger journey of life, encapsulating lessons of love, fear, and belief.

In conclusion, the depth and significance of newly formed emotional bonds in the world of sports provide a window into the complexities of human relationships. These connections, rooted in initial impressions and beliefs, evolve to profoundly impact individuals' lives and beliefs. As a coach, I have learned that these early emotional connections are not just about building a successful team; they are about nurturing growth, fostering resilience, and leaving a lasting impact on the lives of those I mentor. As we continue to explore the themes of belief, fear, and love, let us not underestimate the power of these early bonds in shaping our journeys and defining our destinies.

The Omnipresence of Fear

Chapter 7

I have encountered the omnipresence of fear just as much as you. This emotion, often perceived as a negative force, has revealed itself as a constant companion in the human journey. It is an underlying current in our decision-making, a whisper in moments of doubt, and a loud echo in times of uncertainty.

Fear, I have come to realize, is not merely an obstacle; it is a fundamental aspect of the human experience. In the world of basketball, fear presents itself in various forms: the fear of failure, the fear of not living up to expectations, the fear of injury, or the fear of losing. These fears are not just fleeting thoughts; they are powerful forces that can shape a player's mindset and approach to the game.

Yet, fear extends beyond the court. In life, we face fears that are more intricate and profound. Fear of loss, fear of change, fear of the unknown - these are universal experiences that resonate with each of us at different stages of our lives. They challenge us, test our resilience, and often, force us to confront aspects of ourselves we would rather not see.

However, the omnipresence of fear is not a call for despair. Instead, it is an invitation to understand and engage with this emotion in a way that fosters growth and learning. In my coaching career, I have seen how acknowledging and addressing fear can lead to breakthroughs in performance and personal development. When a player confronts their fear of failure, they often discover a well of inner strength and a newfound confidence in their abilities.

The role of fear in shaping our beliefs and choices is significant. It is a powerful motivator, compelling us to act, to protect, and sometimes, to retreat. The decisions we make, both on and off the court, are often influenced by our fears - conscious or unconscious. Recognizing this influence is crucial in understanding our actions and reactions.

As I reflect on my journey, I recognize that my beliefs and choices have been significantly molded by my fears. The fear of not succeeding as a coach led me to continuously seek improvement and innovation. The fear of not making a meaningful impact pushed me to invest deeply in the lives of my players. These fears, while challenging, were also catalysts for my growth and success.

In navigating the omnipresence of fear, it is essential to strike a balance between caution and courage. Fear should not be the sole driver of our decisions, but it should not be ignored either. It requires a delicate dance of acknowledging its presence, understanding its roots, and making informed choices that align with our values and aspirations.

The omnipresence of fear in our lives is a truth that cannot be denied. It weaves through our experiences, influencing our beliefs, actions, and the paths we choose. As a coach, mentor, and individual, I have learned that engaging with fear, rather than fleeing from it, leads to a deeper understanding of ourselves and a more authentic way of living. Let this chapter be a reminder of the power of fear - not as a hindrance, but as a guide towards greater self-awareness and fulfillment in our personal and professional lives.

Fear's Role in Shaping Decisions and Actions

Fear weaves its threads both subtly and prominently, influencing our decisions and actions in profound ways. As a basketball coach, I've seen fear manifest in the eyes of players facing crucial moments in a game, and I've felt it myself, standing on the sidelines, decisions weighing heavily. Fear, in its essence, is not just an emotional response; it's a pivotal force in the decision-making process.

Understanding how fear influences our decisions is crucial. It often acts as a barrier, holding us back from taking risks or stepping out of our comfort zones. In basketball, this might mean a player hesitates to take a game-winning shot due to fear of missing. In life, it could be the fear of rejection that stops us from pursuing a dream job or a relationship.

Fear skews our perception of risk and reward, leading us to choose safety over growth.

However, fear's impact on behavior and actions isn't always negative. It can also be a protective mechanism, cautioning us against genuine threats and guiding us to make safer, more considered choices. The key is in recognizing when fear is serving a protective purpose and when it is hindering our progress.

Overcoming fear-based decision-making is a challenge that requires both self-awareness and strategy. As a coach, I often employ techniques to help players manage their fears. This includes visualization exercises, focusing on past successes to boost confidence, and creating a supportive team environment where fears can be openly discussed and addressed.

Similarly, in life, we can tackle fear by confronting it head-on. This might mean gradually exposing ourselves to the things that scare us, seeking support from others, or simply acknowledging our fears and examining their origins. Understanding that fear is a natural part of the human experience can help us approach it with more compassion and less judgment.

The strategies for dealing with fear are as diverse as the fears themselves. Some may find solace in meditation or mindfulness, learning to live in the present moment and reducing anxiety about the future. Others might turn to professional help, such as therapy, to unpack deep-seated fears and learn coping mechanisms.

Fear's role in shaping our decisions and actions is undeniable. It is a powerful force that can either paralyze us or propel us forward, depending on how we engage with it. As we continue through this chapter and in our lives, let's remember that fear, while omnipresent, doesn't have to dictate our path. By understanding and managing our fears, we open the door to more authentic and fulfilling lives, on and off the court. The journey through fear is not about elimination but about integration and balance, turning what once held us back into something that can, ultimately, drive us forward.

The Dichotomy of Love and Fear

In the complex dance of human emotions, love and fear often emerge as the dominant forces, each playing a critical role in shaping our behavior and decisions. As a coach, I have observed the intricate ways these emotions interact, sometimes in harmony and at other times in conflict, within the hearts of my players and within myself.

Love and fear, while seemingly opposite, have a paradoxical relationship. They coexist and, at times, even fuel each other. Consider the love a player has for the game, intertwined with the fear of not performing well. This fear can either cripple their ability to play or, conversely, can heighten their focus and drive, fueled by their love for basketball. Similarly, in life, the love for a person or a dream can be accompanied by the fear of loss or failure, creating a complex emotional landscape.

In moments where love and fear coexist, they can lead to profound personal growth. The love for the game pushes players to confront their fears, to step onto the court despite the risk of defeat. This confrontation is where resilience is built and character is forged. It is in these moments that players often discover their true potential, learning that the presence of fear does not diminish the power of their love for the game.

However, the conflict between love and fear can also lead to turmoil. When fear overshadows love, it can lead to avoidance, missed opportunities, and regret. It can prevent players from taking crucial shots or stop individuals from pursuing their passions. In these scenarios, fear becomes a barrier, blocking the path that love lays out.

Finding a balance between love and fear is crucial for personal development. Embracing love can provide the courage to face our fears, while acknowledging fear can keep our love grounded and realistic. This balance is not static; it is a continuous process of negotiation and adjustment, shaped by experiences and introspection.

I have seen the transformative power of this balance in my coaching career. Players who have learned to channel their fear into a driving force, guided by their love for the game, often achieve remarkable growth. They learn to embrace the challenges, to appreciate the journey, and to find joy in their pursuit, regardless of the outcome.

In our lives, the dichotomy of love and fear plays out in various ways. The fear of losing a loved one can deepen our appreciation and love for them. The fear of failing at a dream can fuel our passion and determination to succeed. It is in navigating this dichotomy that we learn about ourselves, our values, and our capacity to overcome challenges.

The interplay of love and fear is a central theme in the human experience. It influences our decisions, shapes our actions, and molds our character. As we journey through life, let us be mindful of this delicate balance. Let us embrace love to overcome fear, and let us acknowledge fear to deepen our understanding of love. This dance between love and fear is not just a struggle; it is an opportunity for growth, discovery, and ultimately, a more fulfilling life.

Prevalence of Fear-Based Decision Making

On the court, fear manifests in decisions made under pressure, in hesitation, and in the reluctance to take risks. This same pattern is mirrored in society where fear influences choices on a grand scale, from career paths to personal relationships. Fear of failure, rejection, and uncertainty can lead to conservative decision-making, often at the expense of innovation and growth. It's a cycle that perpetuates safe choices, limiting potential and stifling creativity.

The impact of fear on societal norms and personal choices is significant. Societally, fear can lead to conformity, where individuals feel pressured to align with perceived norms rather than pursuing their unique paths.

Personally, fear-based decisions can result in missed opportunities and regrets, as individuals opt for the safer, more predictable options.

Recognizing and addressing fear-based thinking is crucial for breaking this cycle. It involves a conscious effort to identify fear's influence on our decisions and to challenge the automatic responses it triggers. This process requires introspection and, often, a willingness to step out of comfort zones.

One effective way to combat fear-based decision making is through fostering environments that encourage risk-taking and embrace failure as a learning opportunity. In basketball, this means creating a team culture that values effort and growth over mere wins or losses. Similarly, in society, it means promoting values that prioritize exploration, innovation, and personal authenticity over rigid adherence to societal expectations.

Another strategy is to develop resilience to fear. This can be achieved through experiences that challenge us, teaching us to cope with uncertainty and setbacks. Whether it's a player learning to handle the pressure of a critical game or an individual navigating the complexities of life choices, building resilience is key to overcoming fear's paralyzing effects.

In conclusion, the prevalence of fear-based decision making in our society and personal lives is a challenge that requires collective and individual efforts to overcome. By recognizing fear's role, creating supportive environments, and building resilience, we can pave the way for more courageous, authentic decision-making. As we move forward in this chapter and in our lives, let us strive to understand fear's dynamics, confront it with courage, and make choices that reflect our true aspirations and values. The journey through fear is not one of avoidance, but of engagement and transformation, leading to a more empowered and fulfilling life.

Conquering the Shadows

As I close this chapter on the omnipresence of fear, I stand firm in the conviction that understanding and confronting our fears is not just essential, it is transformative. Fear, a constant in our lives, shapes our decisions and actions in profound ways, both on the basketball court and in the vast arena of life. However, acknowledging fear's presence is the first step in transforming it from a hindrance into a tool for growth and empowerment.

In basketball, as in life, fear of failure often looms large. But it's in the heart of this fear that we find the seeds of resilience and strength. Players who confront their fear of missing the crucial shot often become the ones who take the game-winning leap. Similarly, in life, when we face our fears - be it fear of change, rejection, or the unknown - we open the door to new possibilities, to growth, and to a deeper understanding of who we are.

The role of fear in shaping our decisions and actions is undeniable. It can act as a barrier, holding us back from achieving our full potential. Yet, it's also a powerful motivator, compelling us to act and to protect. The key is to recognize when fear is limiting us and when it's guiding us towards making more informed, conscious choices. This understanding comes from introspection, courage, and a willingness to step into the unknown.

Throughout my coaching career, I have employed various strategies to help players manage their fears. Visualization, focusing on past successes, and cultivating a supportive environment are just a few ways to mitigate fear's grip. Similarly, in our personal lives, confronting our fears, seeking support, and engaging in practices like mindfulness can help us navigate through fear's murky waters.

Fear's prevalence in decision-making, both at societal and individual levels, is a testament to its power. But it's in recognizing and addressing this fear-based thinking that we can begin to break the cycle of safety and limitation. By fostering environments that encourage risk-taking, by building resilience, and by confronting fear head-on, we empower ourselves to make choices that align with our true aspirations.

As we conclude this chapter, let us remember that the journey through fear is not about elimination but about integration and balance. It's about turning what once held us back into a source of strength and motivation. Let's embrace the dichotomy of love and fear, understanding that in their dance lies the potential for profound personal growth and fulfillment.

Fear, in all its forms, is a part of our journey - a journey that challenges us, molds us, and ultimately, leads us towards a more authentic and fulfilling life. As we move forward, let's carry with us the lessons learned from fear, using them as a compass to guide our decisions, to shape our actions, and to live a life driven not by fear, but by the courage to face it.

In this chapter, we have delved deep into the heart of fear, understanding its omnipresence and influence. Now, as we step into the next phase of our journey, let us do so with the knowledge that fear, though ever-present, is a force that we can understand, manage, and ultimately use to propel ourselves towards our highest potential. Let this be our legacy - not that we lived without fear, but that we lived fully, bravely, and authentically, in spite of it.

Liberation through Overcoming Fear of Death

Chapter 8

As we embark on the exploration of this profound chapter, it's crucial to acknowledge that the fear of death is perhaps the most primal of all fears. Throughout my years of coaching, I've witnessed firsthand how this fear, though often unspoken, casts a long shadow over decisions, actions, and beliefs. As Coach Ron Moncrief, my journey through the realms of basketball and life has taught me that confronting and overcoming the fear of death is not just about grappling with the end of life, but about embracing the fullness of our existence.

In the microcosm of basketball, the fear of death manifests metaphorically. Players often confront what feels like life-and-death situations in the game - the final shot, the decisive play. These moments, though not literally matters of life and death, carry a weight that echoes that ultimate fear. Overcoming this fear on the court has been a transformative experience for many players, leading them not only to athletic triumphs but also to personal liberation.

But it's off the court where the fear of death takes on a more profound and existential dimension. This fear, deeply ingrained in our psyche, often operates in the background, subtly influencing our life choices. It can lead to a cautious approach to life, a reluctance to take risks, and a tendency to cling to safety and certainty. However, true liberation comes when we confront this fear head-on, when we realize that acknowledging the inevitability of death can be a powerful motivator to live more fully and authentically.

In my personal journey, the fear of death has been a silent companion, a reminder of the finite nature of life. It has taught me to value each moment, to embrace each opportunity, and to live with a sense of purpose. The realization that our time is limited can be a profound motivator to pursue our passions, to connect deeply with others, and to leave a meaningful impact in the world.

Overcoming the fear of death also involves a shift in perspective. It's about seeing life not as a journey towards an end but as a series of moments to be cherished and lived to the fullest. This perspective fosters a sense of gratitude, a deeper appreciation for the present, and a commitment to making each day count.

In the context of coaching and mentoring, addressing the fear of death has often involved helping players to focus on the here and now, to give their best in each game, each play, without the paralyzing fear of what might go wrong. This approach can be applied to life as well. By focusing on the present, we liberate ourselves from the fear of an unknown future, allowing us to engage more fully with the richness of life.

The liberation that comes from overcoming the fear of death is not about denying or escaping the reality of our mortality. Rather, it's about embracing it as a fundamental part of the human experience. This acceptance opens up a space for courage, for joy, and for a deeper engagement with life.

As we delve deeper into this chapter, let us reflect on how the fear of death shapes our beliefs, actions, and decisions. Let us explore ways to confront and transcend this fear, not just to overcome it, but to use it as a catalyst for living more fully, more bravely, and with greater authenticity. In the end, the journey towards overcoming the fear of death is a journey towards embracing life in all its complexity, beauty, and impermanence.

The Transformative Power of Confronting Mortality

In the journey of life, especially in the high-stakes world of competitive sports, the confrontation with our own mortality often lurks in the background, a subtle but pervasive presence. As a coach and mentor, I have observed that acknowledging and accepting our mortality can be a catalyst for profound personal growth. This realization, while initially daunting, can lead to a psychological shift, altering our perception of life, our priorities, and our values.

When one confronts their own finitude, a transformation begins. It's like stepping out of a fog into clarity. This awareness brings into sharp focus the preciousness of each moment and the impermanence of our existence. In my coaching experience, when players grasp the transience of their athletic careers, they often find a renewed vigor and passion for the game. They play not just to win but to savor the experience, to make the most of their time on the court.

This psychological shift also influences life's priorities and values. The realization of our mortality can lead to a reevaluation of what truly matters. In my own life, this awareness has made me prioritize relationships, personal growth, and the impact I can have on others over material success or fleeting achievements. It has taught me to value the journey itself, with all its ups and downs, rather than just the destination.

Moreover, confronting mortality can be a liberating experience. It frees us from the shackles of trivial concerns and societal pressures, allowing us to live more authentically. We start to make choices based on what genuinely resonates with our inner selves rather than being driven by external expectations or the fear of judgment. For a basketball player, this might mean playing the game in a way that is true to their style and values, rather than conforming to a prescribed role. For an individual, it could mean pursuing a path that is aligned with their true passions and aspirations.

However, this confrontation with mortality is not a one-time event but an ongoing process. It requires continuous reflection and courage to face the unknown. In my role as a coach, I encourage players to embrace this process, to use it as a source of strength and motivation. We discuss the importance of living fully in the present, of giving their all in every practice and game, not out of fear of the end but in celebration of the now.

The transformative power of confronting our mortality is a central theme in the human experience. It challenges us to live with intention, to cherish each moment, and to pursue what truly matters. As we move forward in this chapter and in life, let us embrace this confrontation with openness and courage. Let it be a reminder of the fleeting nature of our existence and a call to live our lives with purpose, passion, and authenticity. Let the acknowledgment of our mortality not be a source of fear, but a wellspring of inspiration, guiding us towards a life of depth, meaning, and fulfillment.

Freedom from Fear and Its Effects on Life Choices

When the fear of death diminishes, a remarkable shift occurs in how we approach life. The boundaries we once saw as impenetrable start to dissolve, and the risks we avoided become stepping stones to a fuller, more authentic existence. In basketball, this can be seen when a player, who once played cautiously for fear of making mistakes, begins to play boldly, taking calculated risks that often lead to spectacular results. They start to play 'their' game, not constrained by fear, but driven by passion and authenticity.

This shift also profoundly impacts decision-making. Choices that were once guided by the avoidance of failure or rejection now become opportunities for growth and exploration. We begin to make decisions that align more closely with our true selves, our values, and our aspirations. This alignment creates a sense of congruence and integrity in our lives, leading to deeper satisfaction and fulfillment.

Overcoming the fear of death empowers us to live authentically. It peels away the layers of societal expectations, self-doubt, and conformity, allowing our true selves to emerge. This authenticity is not just about being true to ourselves but also about connecting more genuinely with others. In the realm of coaching, this means fostering an environment where players feel safe to express themselves, to take risks, and to grow not only as athletes but as individuals.

The liberation from the fear of death is not about recklessness but about thoughtful courage. It involves making choices that are mindful of the risks but are also guided by the potential for growth and fulfillment. It's about recognizing that our time is limited and that living cautiously can mean not living at all.

As we get close to wrapping up this chapter on the liberation through overcoming the fear of death, let us carry forward the understanding that this liberation is not an end but a beginning. It is the start of a journey towards living more boldly, authentically, and purposefully. Let us use this newfound freedom not just to enhance our own lives but to inspire and uplift those around us. Let the knowledge of our mortality be not a source of fear, but a beacon that guides us to make the most of every moment we have. As we step into the future, let us do so with the courage to face our fears, the wisdom to make empowering choices, and the heart to live fully and fearlessly.

The Release from Pain and Embarrassment

As we delve deeper into understanding the fear of death in Chapter 8 of "Liberation through Overcoming Fear of Death," a significant realization unfolds: accepting death not only liberates us from its fear but also alleviates the anxieties surrounding pain and embarrassment. These, too, are fears deeply rooted in our psyche, often holding us back in various arenas of life, including sports and personal endeavors.

I've seen how the fear of physical pain or the dread of embarrassment can significantly hinder performance and limit potential. Athletes might shy away from challenging plays due to fear of injury or avoid taking decisive actions in a game to escape potential ridicule. Similarly, in our personal lives, the dread of embarrassment can prevent us from expressing our true selves or taking bold steps towards our goals.

The acceptance of death, however, brings about a profound shift. When we acknowledge and accept the inevitability of our end, we begin to see pain and embarrassment in a new light. They become transient experiences rather than defining ones. This perspective transforms our approach to life's challenges. In basketball, for instance, players who accept the impermanence of life and career might play with more freedom and resilience, viewing potential pain and embarrassment as temporary hurdles rather than insurmountable barriers.

Moreover, considering death as a natural and unifying experience changes our outlook. It creates a sense of solidarity and empathy among us. Understanding that we all share the same fate can diminish the impact of pain and embarrassment. On the basketball court, this realization fosters a team spirit where players support each other, knowing that everyone is vulnerable to the same fears and uncertainties.

This awareness also influences how we deal with life's challenges. When we diminish our fear of death, pain, and embarrassment, our decision-making process evolves. We become more inclined to take calculated risks, embrace new opportunities, and live authentically. This bravery to face life head-on, undeterred by the fear of temporary discomfort or societal judgment, leads to a richer, more fulfilling existence.

In essence, the liberation from the fear of death offers us a freedom that extends far beyond the mere acceptance of our mortality. It frees us from the shackles of pain and embarrassment, allowing us to live more fully in the present. It encourages us to embrace our vulnerabilities, to recognize them as part of the shared human experience, and to use them as catalysts for growth and connection.

As we conclude this chapter, let us carry forward the understanding that confronting our mortality is not just about coming to terms with the end of life. It's about embracing life in its entirety, with all its joys, pains, and embarrassments. Let this realization inspire us to live with courage, to take risks, and to make choices that align with our deepest values and aspirations. Let us remember that in the grand scheme of life, pain and embarrassment are but fleeting moments, and it is in our power to rise above them and live a life marked by bravery, authenticity, and profound fulfillment.

Manifestations of Fear in Life

Chapter 9

In this chapter, we will examine the multifaceted manifestations of fear in life, a theme that resonates deeply with my experiences as Coach Ron Moncrief. Over the years, coaching basketball has not just been about the sport; it's been a journey into understanding the human psyche, especially the role of fear. Fear, as I've come to learn, wears many masks and affects our lives in a myriad of ways.

On the basketball court, fear often appears as performance anxiety, the dread of making a mistake, or the apprehension of not meeting expectations. These fears can be palpable, influencing a player's every move, dictating their decisions on the court. It's a battle not just against the opposing team, but also against one's own inner demons.

But fear extends far beyond the boundaries of the basketball court. In life, its manifestations are even more diverse and complex. Fear can show up as reluctance to embrace change, as resistance to new experiences, or as hesitation to express one's true self. It can manifest in our relationships, our career choices, and our personal growth. At times, it is a subtle undercurrent, influencing our decisions without us even realizing it.

One of the most common manifestations of fear I've observed is the fear of failure. This fear can paralyze, leading to inaction or avoidance. It can stop a talented player from taking the decisive shot, or prevent an individual from pursuing a dream. The irony, however, is that in trying to avoid failure, we often miss out on opportunities for success and learning.

Another significant manifestation is the fear of rejection or not belonging. This fear can be seen in players who conform to group dynamics, even if it means suppressing their unique talents or beliefs. In our lives, this fear can lead us to make choices that align with societal expectations rather than our true desires, leading to a life of conformity and unfulfilled potential.

The fear of the unknown is yet another manifestation that I've encountered. It's the uncertainty about the future, the ambiguity of the unknown that can be daunting. This fear can keep players, and people in general, tethered to their comfort zones, inhibiting growth and exploration.

As a coach, I have learned that acknowledging and confronting these fears is the first step towards overcoming them. It's about creating a safe environment where players feel empowered to face their fears, to take risks, and to learn from their experiences. This approach is equally applicable in life. Confronting our fears, be it fear of failure, rejection, or the unknown, requires courage and a willingness to be vulnerable.

The journey of overcoming fear is a continuous process. It involves introspection, understanding the roots of our fears, and actively working to mitigate their influence on our lives. It's about shifting our perspective from viewing fear as an adversary to seeing it as an opportunity for growth.

The manifestations of fear in life are varied and omnipresent. As we proceed through this chapter, let's delve into the nuances of these fears, understand their impact, and explore strategies to overcome them. Let us remember that it's not about the absence of fear, but about the mastery of it. Embracing this journey can lead to a life of authenticity, courage, and fulfillment, both on and off the basketball court.

Fear of Not Meeting Needs

In the heart of this journey, we confront a fear that is often overlooked yet pervasive - the fear of inadequacy. This fear, rooted in the dread of not being enough or not meeting certain standards, can be a significant driver in our lives. It can shape our self-esteem, influence our life choices, and manifest in various aspects of our existence, such as our careers, relationships, and personal goals.

I have seen this fear in many players. The fear of not being good enough to make the team, to score the winning point, or to meet my expectations. This fear of inadequacy can lead to a crippling pressure that hinders performance. It's a fear that, if not addressed, can permeate into other areas of life, leading to choices and actions driven by a need to prove worthiness, rather than genuine desire or passion.

In careers, the fear of inadequacy often leads to overworking, to taking on more than we can handle in a bid to prove ourselves. It can result in staying in unfulfilling jobs because of the fear of not being capable enough for better opportunities. In relationships, this fear manifests in the need for constant reassurance, in the reluctance to express true feelings, or in staying in unhealthy dynamics due to the fear of not being loved or accepted elsewhere.

The psychological shift that needs to occur to overcome this fear is profound. It involves a journey of self-acceptance, of recognizing and embracing our inherent worth. This journey is not easy. It requires confronting deep-seated beliefs about ourselves and often, challenging societal and cultural narratives that have shaped these beliefs.

One strategy to address this fear is through cultivating self-compassion. This involves being kind to ourselves, acknowledging our humanity, and understanding that imperfection is part of the human experience. It's about changing the internal dialogue from one of criticism and comparison to one of encouragement and support.

Another strategy is seeking authenticity in our actions and choices. This means making decisions based on what truly aligns with our values and aspirations, rather than what we think we should do to feel adequate or accepted. In basketball, this could mean focusing on playing to one's strengths and enjoying the game, rather than obsessing over every mistake or the final score.

Mindfulness practices can also be beneficial in overcoming the fear of inadequacy. These practices help us stay present and grounded, reducing the anxiety about future failures or past mistakes. They encourage a focus on the here and now, allowing us to engage fully in our current actions and interactions.

The fear of not meeting needs, or the fear of inadequacy, is a formidable force in our lives. However, it is not insurmountable. By cultivating self-compassion, seeking authenticity, and practicing mindfulness, we can begin to mitigate this fear's impact. As we move through life, let us strive to understand and overcome this fear, not just for our own sake but to inspire those we lead and mentor. Let the journey of overcoming the fear of inadequacy be one of empowerment, leading us to a life where we are no longer held back by doubts of our worth, but propelled forward by the knowledge of our inherent value.

Navigating the Shadows of Inadequacy

Let's keep examining the realm of fear, particularly the fear of inadequacy, unveils a labyrinth of emotional complexities that profoundly influence the human experience. This fear, often concealed beneath layers of bravado or denial, can be a silent saboteur, impacting the core of our being - our self-esteem, our relationships, and the pursuit of our aspirations. As Coach Ron Moncrief, I've seen this fear not just in the athletes I coach but also as a universal thread that runs through the tapestry of human existence.

At its core, the fear of inadequacy is linked to our self-identity and self-worth. It's a fear that whispers incessantly that we are not enough, that our efforts are insufficient, and that our value is conditional upon external validation. This insidious fear often stems from early life experiences, societal pressures, and cultural norms that dictate a rigid framework of success and acceptance. It's a fear that disguises itself in various forms, sometimes as perfectionism, other times as procrastination, and often as a relentless inner critic that undermines our confidence and potential.

The manifestation of this fear can be seen in various aspects of life. Professionally, it can drive us into a relentless pursuit of achievements, accolades, and recognition, often at the expense of our health, relationships, and inner peace. In our personal lives, it can manifest as an inability to form deep, meaningful relationships, for fear of being seen as inadequate or unworthy. It can also surface in our reluctance to pursue personal goals, hampered by a crippling belief that we are not capable or deserving of achieving them.

Addressing this deep-seated fear requires more than surface-level solutions; it demands a radical transformation of our internal narrative. This transformation begins with the cultivation of self-awareness - a conscious recognition of the patterns and beliefs that fuel our fear of inadequacy. It's about identifying the moments when we diminish our worth, question our capabilities, or allow external standards to define our success.

In the path towards overcoming this fear, self-compassion emerges as a potent tool. It's about replacing self-criticism with kindness, acknowledging our humanity, and understanding that failure and imperfection are intrinsic parts of the human journey. This shift towards self-compassion is transformative, as it allows us to view ourselves through a lens of empathy and understanding, rather than judgment and comparison.

Another pivotal strategy in navigating the shadows of inadequacy is embracing authenticity. This means honoring our true selves, our unique talents, and our individual journey. It's about making choices that resonate with our core values, rather than succumbing to the pressure of societal norms or expectations. Authenticity empowers us to live in alignment with who we truly are, freeing us from the shackles of inadequacy and enabling us to express our fullest potential.

Mindfulness and presence are also vital in this journey. They anchor us in the present moment, reducing the power of past regrets and future anxieties. Through mindfulness, we learn to engage with life as it unfolds, embracing each experience with openness and curiosity, rather than through the lens of fear and inadequacy.

In essence, navigating the shadows of inadequacy is a journey towards self-liberation. It's a path that leads us away from the confines of fear and towards a life of authenticity, courage, and fulfillment. As we embrace this journey, we not only liberate ourselves but also become beacons of inspiration for others. By overcoming the fear of inadequacy, we pave the way for a life rich in self-acceptance, meaningful relationships, and the pursuit of our true passions. Let this chapter be a guidepost in that journey, illuminating the path towards a life where fear no longer dictates our choices, but where our inherent worth and authenticity shine brightly, guiding us towards our true destiny.

The Weight of Attachment: Fear and the Loss of the Valued

Attachment, in its essence, is a natural part of the human condition. We form bonds, we cherish memories, we value possessions - these connections are fundamental to our sense of self and belonging. However, the fear of losing these valued aspects of our lives can lead to a paradoxical situation. On one hand, these attachments enrich our lives, offering joy, meaning, and purpose. On the other hand, the fear of losing them can become a source of constant anxiety and can drive us to behaviors that are counterproductive or even harmful.

In the realm of basketball, this fear manifests in players who might cling too tightly to their status, their image, or their role in the team. The fear of losing these can lead to a resistance to change, reluctance to adapt, or an inability to work collaboratively. In our broader lives, this fear can make us overly possessive in relationships, excessively materialistic, or resistant to life's inevitable changes and losses.

Balancing our value of people and possessions with the fear of losing them is a delicate dance. It requires a conscious effort to appreciate and enjoy what we have, without becoming overly attached or dependent on these for our happiness and sense of self-worth. This balance is not about detachment in the sense of disconnection or indifference. Rather, it's about cultivating a healthy detachment - an understanding that while we value and cherish our connections and possessions, our ultimate well-being does not solely depend on them.

This form of detachment is liberating. It frees us from the cycle of fear and anxiety that comes with over-attachment. It allows us to enjoy our relationships and possessions, to fully engage with them, but without the constant dread of loss overshadowing our experiences. This detachment also fosters resilience, equipping us to face losses and changes with a sense of acceptance and peace, rather than fear and despair.

In coaching, I encourage players to find value in the process, in the learning, and in the growth that comes from the game, rather than just the outcomes or accolades. This approach can be applied to life as well. By finding value in the experiences, the growth, and the connections themselves, rather than just the end results or the permanence of things, we can mitigate the fear of loss.

The role of detachment in managing the fear of losing what is valued is akin to walking a tightrope. It's about maintaining a balance between caring deeply and holding lightly, between valuing greatly and accepting change. As we navigate through this chapter and through life, let us reflect on our attachments and the fear they bring. Let us strive to cultivate a healthy detachment, one that allows us to embrace life fully, to love deeply, but without the heavy chains of fear. Let this journey of finding balance be a transformative one, leading us to a place of greater peace, resilience, and freedom.

Self-Sufficiency and Inner Fulfillment

Chapter 10

In this journey, a pivotal realization I've embraced the profound significance of self-sufficiency and inner fulfillment. These concepts, often sidelined in the pursuit of external achievements and validation, are the bedrock of a life lived with authenticity and contentment. My time on the court and in life has taught me that true strength and happiness emanate from within, not from external accolades or possessions.

Self-sufficiency, in its essence, is not about isolation or egoistic self-reliance. Rather, it's about cultivating an inner resilience and independence of spirit. It's the ability to find contentment and strength within oneself, rather than constantly seeking it from external sources. In basketball, this translates to a player who can motivate themselves, who can find their drive from within, even when external support is lacking. Off the court, it's about navigating life's challenges with a sense of inner confidence and self-reliance.

This concept of self-sufficiency is deeply intertwined with inner fulfillment. Inner fulfillment is not just a fleeting feeling of happiness. It's a profound sense of contentment and peace that comes from living in alignment with one's values and purpose. It's about finding joy in the journey, not just the destination. In the high-pressure environment of competitive sports, finding inner fulfillment means appreciating the growth and learning each game brings, irrespective of the outcome.

The pursuit of self-sufficiency and inner fulfillment often requires a recalibration of our priorities and values. It involves shifting the focus from external validation to internal satisfaction. This shift is not trivial; it challenges the societal norms that equate success with external achievements and possessions. It requires a deep introspection and a willingness to redefine what success and happiness truly mean.

One of the key strategies in cultivating self-sufficiency and inner fulfillment is mindfulness. Mindfulness allows us to connect with our inner selves, to become acutely aware of our thoughts, feelings, and actions. It helps us recognize our intrinsic worth and detach our self-esteem from external accolades. In my coaching, I encourage players to practice mindfulness, to be present in each moment, whether it's a practice session or a championship game. This practice helps them find fulfillment in their effort and presence, rather than just the final score.

Another important aspect is embracing self-compassion. Self-compassion involves treating oneself with kindness and understanding in the face of failures and setbacks. It's about recognizing that imperfection is part of the human experience. Cultivating self-compassion allows us to navigate life's ups and downs with a sense of grace and resilience, finding fulfillment in our journey, regardless of the external circumstances.

The journey towards self-sufficiency and inner fulfillment is a transformative one. It's a path that leads away from the relentless pursuit of external validation and towards a life of authenticity, resilience, and true contentment. As we explore this chapter, let us embrace the principles of mindfulness and self-compassion. Let us redefine success on our own terms and cultivate an inner well of strength and fulfillment. This journey, though challenging, is incredibly rewarding, as it leads to a life where we are not just surviving but thriving, anchored in our inner strength and true to our deepest selves. Let this chapter be a guide in that transformative journey, a journey towards a life of self-sufficiency and inner fulfillment.

Debunking the Need for External Fulfillment

As we delve deeper into the concept of self-sufficiency and inner fulfillment in Chapter 10, it becomes imperative to challenge a deeply ingrained cultural narrative: the notion that true happiness and fulfillment originate from external sources. This idea, perpetuated by societal norms and cultural influences, often leads us on a relentless quest for external validation and achievements. Yet, the essence of genuine contentment lies within, not in the accolades or possessions we accumulate.

In the realm of sports, particularly basketball, the pressure to seek external validation is intense. Players are often judged by their stats, the number of wins, or the accolades they receive. However, this external pursuit can lead to a hollow sense of achievement, where the joy of the game is overshadowed by the need for recognition. The true beauty of sports, and life, is found in the journey, in the personal growth and the love of the game, not merely in the trophies or titles.

The benefits of finding contentment within oneself are immense. It fosters a sense of inner peace and stability that is not easily shaken by external circumstances. This internal fulfillment allows individuals to approach life with a sense of wholeness and self-assurance, leading to decisions and actions that are more aligned with their authentic selves. It also cultivates resilience, enabling individuals to face life's challenges with equanimity and strength.

However, detaching from the need for external validation is not a simple task. It requires a conscious unlearning of societal and cultural conditioning that equates success and worthiness with external achievements. This conditioning is pervasive, often reinforced by media, societal norms, and even our upbringing. It shapes our perception of success and happiness, leading us to believe that these can only be attained through external means.

To counteract this conditioning, it is crucial to engage in introspection and mindful practices. Mindfulness helps us stay present and grounded, allowing us to find joy and fulfillment in the here and now, rather than in some elusive future achievement. It teaches us to appreciate the intrinsic value of our experiences and our inherent worth, independent of external validation.

Moreover, embracing a mindset of self-compassion is vital in this journey. Self-compassion involves treating ourselves with kindness and understanding, especially in the face of failures or setbacks. It allows us to view our experiences, not as measures of our worth, but as opportunities for growth and learning. This perspective shifts our focus from external approval to internal development and self-acceptance.

Debunking the need for external fulfillment is a crucial step towards living a life of authenticity and contentment. It involves recognizing the cultural and societal factors that promote external validation and consciously choosing to find fulfillment within. As we progress through Chapter 10, let's embrace this journey towards self-sufficiency and inner fulfillment. Let us seek to redefine success and happiness on our terms, finding strength and satisfaction in our inner selves. This path, though challenging, leads to a life of genuine fulfillment, where our sense of worth and happiness is not contingent on external factors, but rooted in our own inner resilience and authenticity.

Recognizing the Inner Source of Joy

In our pursuit of self-sufficiency and inner fulfillment, a crucial aspect to explore is the concept of internal sources of happiness and fulfillment. As we journey through Chapter 10, it's essential to understand that the wellspring of true joy resides within us. This realization is transformative, especially in a world where external achievements and possessions are often mistaken for the source of true happiness.

I've seen the importance of recognizing and nurturing the inner source of joy, both on and off the court. In basketball, the most fulfilled players are often those who find joy in the process of the game itself, not just in winning or recognition. They derive pleasure from the act of playing, improving, and being part of a team. This inner source of joy sustains them, even when external rewards are not forthcoming.

The practices that can help individuals connect with their inner joy are varied but profoundly impactful. One such practice is mindfulness, which I've integrated into my coaching. Mindfulness allows players and individuals to focus on the present moment, to fully engage in the current activity, and to find joy in the here and now, rather than constantly seeking it in future achievements or external validation.

Another practice is the cultivation of gratitude. By recognizing and appreciating what we have, rather than fixating on what we lack or what we desire, we can tap into a deep sense of contentment and joy. This perspective shift can profoundly impact our overall well-being and approach to life.

The long-term effects of relying on internal rather than external sources for happiness are transformative. When individuals learn to derive joy from within, they become less dependent on external circumstances for their happiness. This independence leads to greater emotional stability and resilience, as their well-being is not at the mercy of fluctuating external factors.

Moreover, internal sources of happiness often lead to more sustainable and authentic ways of living. When our actions are driven by internal fulfillment rather than external validation, we make choices that are more aligned with our true selves and values. This alignment brings a sense of integrity and authenticity to our lives, enhancing our overall satisfaction and sense of purpose.

In my personal journey, embracing the inner source of joy has been liberating. It has allowed me to appreciate the beauty of the present moment, to find fulfillment in my role as a coach, and to live a life that is not dictated by societal measures of success but guided by my values and passions.

Our exploration into self-sufficiency and inner fulfillment calls us to recognize and nurture our inner source of joy. By practicing mindfulness, cultivating gratitude, and seeking internal fulfillment, we can build lives of authentic happiness and contentment. This internal focus not only enhances our personal well-being but also empowers us to lead and inspire others from a place of genuine joy and fulfillment. Let us continue this journey, embracing the inner source of joy as the foundation for a life lived with purpose, passion, and profound contentment.

Redirecting Focus from the Trivial to the Essential

In the high-paced, achievement-oriented world of basketball, as well as in the broader spectrum of life, it's easy to become entangled in the superficial pursuits of status, material possessions, and societal approval. These pursuits, though seemingly rewarding in the short term, often lead to a sense of emptiness and a relentless craving for more. The true essence of life, however, lies in focusing on deeper, more meaningful goals - those that align with our core values and inner desires.

Prioritizing what truly matters involves a conscious decision to evaluate and realign our life's objectives. It requires us to ask ourselves tough questions about the nature of our ambitions and the sources of our happiness. Are we chasing goals that truly fulfill us, or are we merely succumbing to external pressures and societal norms? The shift from chasing external validation to cultivating internal satisfaction can be transformative.

This shift in focus has a profound impact on our mental well-being. When we begin to value and work towards goals that resonate with our true selves, we experience a sense of authenticity and purpose that external achievements can never provide. This authenticity leads to a deeper sense of fulfillment and a more balanced, peaceful state of mind.

The benefits of this shift are multifold. It fosters a sense of inner peace and contentment, as our actions and goals become congruent with our personal values and beliefs. It enhances our resilience, as we become less dependent on external circumstances for our sense of self-worth and happiness. Additionally, this realignment allows us to cultivate richer, more meaningful relationships, as we interact with others from a place of authenticity and self-assurance.

In my coaching career, I have always emphasized the importance of focusing on the personal growth and development of each player, rather than just the outcome of the game. This approach not only improves their performance but also instills a sense of intrinsic motivation and satisfaction in their endeavors. Similarly, in life, when we focus on personal growth, meaningful relationships, and contributions to the community, we experience a deeper sense of fulfillment that transcends the fleeting pleasure of superficial achievements.

In conclusion, Chapter 10 of our journey underscores the significance of redirecting our focus from the trivial to the essential. By embracing this shift, we open ourselves to a life of deeper meaning, genuine happiness, and authentic fulfillment. Let this chapter serve as a reminder to continually assess and realign our priorities, to focus on what truly matters, and to live a life that is not just successful by societal standards but is truly enriching and rewarding in the deepest sense. Let us embrace the journey towards a life that prioritizes the essential, for it is in this journey that we find the true essence of self-sufficiency and inner fulfillment.

The Art of Being the Truest Self

Chapter 11

In this profound journey of exploring belief, fear, and love, a pivotal realization has emerged, one that has been both my compass and anchor as Coach Ron Moncrief. Chapter 11 delves into what I consider the pinnacle of personal growth and fulfillment: the art of being the truest self. This concept, though seemingly simple, is a formidable undertaking in a world rife with masks and facades.

The essence of being one's truest self is not merely about authenticity; it's about peeling back the layers of societal expectations, personal insecurities, and ingrained beliefs to uncover the core of who we truly are. In my years of coaching young athletes, I have witnessed the transformative power of embracing one's true identity. It's like watching a player step out of the shadows into their full potential, not just on the court, but in every aspect of life.

The journey to becoming our truest selves starts with self-awareness. It's about having the courage to look inward, to question our motives, desires, and fears. Are we pursuing goals that genuinely resonate with us, or are we chasing dreams imposed upon us by others? On the basketball court, this might mean a player recognizing their unique style and strengths, rather than trying to fit into a mold that doesn't align with who they are.

Another crucial aspect of this journey is the willingness to embrace vulnerability. Often, we hide behind facades for fear of judgment or rejection. However, true strength lies in showing our real selves, complete with our flaws and uncertainties. As a coach, I've always encouraged my players to be vulnerable, to express their true feelings and fears. This openness not only fosters stronger team bonds but also allows individuals to grow in authenticity and self-acceptance.

Moreover, being our truest selves involves letting go of the fear of judgment. In a culture obsessed with appearances and social approval, this fear can be paralyzing. It takes immense courage to stand apart from the crowd, to be different, to be true. But the freedom that comes with this courage is unparalleled. It's the freedom to live life on our own terms, to make choices that fulfill us deeply, and to express our truest selves without apology.

The art of being the truest self also calls for a redefinition of success. Success is no longer about external accolades or achievements; it's about inner satisfaction and peace. It's about living in a way that aligns with our deepest values and brings us joy. This redefinition is not a rejection of ambition but a redirection towards goals that genuinely matter to us.

In the realm of basketball, embracing one's truest self can lead to a more fulfilling and enjoyable experience of the game. Players who understand and accept their true selves play with more passion, creativity, and resilience. They are not weighed down by the burden of expectations but are uplifted by the joy of being who they truly are.

In conclusion, Chapter 11 - The Art of Being the Truest Self - is a call to embark on the most rewarding journey of all: the journey to self-discovery and authenticity. It's a journey that transcends the basketball court and permeates every facet of life. As we tread this path, let us do so with courage, vulnerability, and an unwavering commitment to our true selves. Let us redefine success, embrace our uniqueness, and live life not as a race for external validation but as an expression of our deepest truths. In doing so, we not only find fulfillment and joy but also become beacons of inspiration for others to discover and embrace their truest selves.

Embracing and Being the Source of One's Existence

Self-reliance and autonomy are not mere concepts; they are the very essence of being the source of one's existence. In my coaching career, I've emphasized to my players that while external guidance and support are valuable, the true power to shape their destiny lies within them. This realization fosters a profound sense of responsibility and empowerment. It's the understanding that the choices we make, the paths we tread, and the lives we lead are a direct reflection of our inner beliefs and actions.

The journey of self-discovery and acceptance is a critical component of this process. It's a path fraught with challenges and introspection, requiring us to confront our deepest fears, question our long-held beliefs, and ultimately, discover the essence of who we truly are. This journey is never linear or easy. It involves moments of doubt, periods of reflection, and a continuous reevaluation of our values and purpose. However, the reward of this journey is immeasurable - a life lived with authenticity and integrity.

In the context of basketball, I've seen players who embrace self-reliance transform their game. They're not just playing; they're expressing themselves, using basketball as a canvas to showcase their inner strength and creativity. These players understand that their performance on the court is a manifestation of their inner state and that true mastery of the game comes from within.

The impact of being the source of one's existence on personal growth is significant. It shifts the locus of control from the external world to the internal self. This shift is empowering. It means that our happiness, our success, and our fulfillment are not contingent on external validation or circumstances but are a result of our internal state and actions. This realization is liberating and fosters a resilience that is not easily shaken by external factors.

However, embracing this role as the architect of our existence comes with its set of responsibilities. It means taking ownership of our actions, our decisions, and their consequences. It requires a level of self-awareness and honesty that can sometimes be uncomfortable but is always enlightening.

"The Art of Being the Truest Self," challenges us to recognize and embrace our role as the source of our existence. It urges us to embark on the journey of self-discovery and acceptance, to cultivate self-reliance and autonomy, and to understand the profound impact of these on our personal growth. As we navigate through this chapter and our lives, let us embrace the power we hold within to shape our destiny. Let us recognize that being the truest self is not just about authenticity; it's about acknowledging and embracing our role as the creators of our life's narrative. This recognition is the first step towards a life of fulfillment, purpose, and profound self-awareness.

The Journey Within: Crafting Our Existence

This chapter extends beyond mere self-discovery and acceptance; it's an invitation to recognize and harness our inner power as the primary architects of our lives. It's about embracing the extraordinary journey of becoming our own source - the source of our strength, our choices, and ultimately, our life's trajectory.

I've learned that the journey to self-reliance is not just about being independent in actions but also about developing an autonomous mindset. It's about cultivating a mental fortitude that doesn't waver in the face of external pressures or opinions. This form of self-reliance is about building an unshakeable core that guides our decisions and actions, based on our deepest convictions and values, rather than external influences or fleeting trends.

The path to embodying this autonomy is intricate and demands a continuous commitment to introspection and self-evaluation. It's about persistently questioning our motivations, unraveling the layers of our identity, and aligning our actions with our true selves. This journey is strewn with moments of self-doubt, uncertainty, and profound realizations, yet each step forward enriches us, making us more aligned with our core essence.

In the realm of basketball, the concept of being one's source is vividly manifested. Players who tap into their inner resources develop a unique resilience and creativity on the court. They play not just with physical skill but with a mental sharpness and emotional intelligence that sets them apart. Their game becomes an extension of their inner world, reflecting their personal journey of growth and self-realization.

The significance of being the architect of one's existence on personal development is immense. It instills a sense of agency and purpose, shifting the dynamics of how we perceive and interact with the world around us. When we realize that we hold the reins to our happiness and success, we begin to make choices that are more authentic and fulfilling. This shift from external dependence to internal empowerment has far-reaching implications on our well-being and life satisfaction.

However, this shift also implies a profound level of responsibility and accountability. Embracing our role as the source of our existence means owning up to our choices, our mistakes, and their outcomes. It requires a level of maturity and wisdom to accept and learn from our experiences, using them as stepping stones for growth and development.

In this chapter, we delve into the transformative potential of recognizing and nurturing our inner source. We explore how this inner journey enriches every aspect of our lives, fostering a sense of authenticity, purpose, and fulfillment. We discuss the practices that aid in this journey, such as reflective contemplation, mindful living, and cultivating emotional intelligence.

By embracing our role as the creators of our existence, we open ourselves to a life of genuine fulfillment and profound self-discovery. This chapter is an invitation to each reader to embark on this transformative journey, to explore the depths of their being, and to emerge as individuals who not only know themselves truly but also possess the courage and conviction to live authentically and purposefully.

Finding Perfection in Imperfection

It's time now to examine a profound aspect of this journey: seeing the perfection in one's journey and self, despite the inherent imperfections. This concept is a radical departure from the relentless pursuit of flawlessness that pervades our society. It's about embracing the beauty and learning that reside in every step of our journey, including the missteps and detours.

In my experience as Coach Ron Moncrief, I've observed how the pressure to be perfect can be crippling, both on and off the basketball court. Players often grapple with the fear of making mistakes, haunted by the notion that perfection is the only path to success. However, the truth is far more liberating. Each mistake, each challenge, and each setback is an integral part of our growth. They are not detriments to our journey but invaluable lessons that shape us into more resilient, empathetic, and authentic individuals.

Embracing one's imperfections is not about settling for mediocrity; it's about recognizing that the pursuit of perfection is an unrealistic and unattainable goal. It's about understanding that our flaws and imperfections are what make us uniquely ourselves. They add depth and richness to our character and allow us to connect with others on a more genuine level. On the court, when players accept their imperfections, they play more freely, unburdened by the fear of judgment. They can fully immerse themselves in the game, enjoying every moment, regardless of the outcome.

This perspective of finding beauty in every step of our journey fosters a profound sense of self-compassion. It allows us to be kinder to ourselves, to acknowledge our efforts, and to celebrate our progress, no matter how small.

Self-compassion is a critical component of personal growth. It enables us to navigate the ups and downs of life with a sense of grace and understanding, rather than harsh self-criticism.

The impact of this mindset on our overall well-being is transformative. When we shift our focus from striving for perfection to appreciating our journey, including the imperfections, we open ourselves to a more fulfilling and satisfying life. We are no longer chained to the unending quest for perfection but are free to explore, experiment, and experience life in all its complexity.

In conclusion, Chapter 11 encourages us to find the perfection in our imperfections and to see the beauty in every step of our journey. It's a call to embrace our true selves, flaws and all, and to appreciate the unique path each of us is on. As we continue on this journey of self-discovery and authenticity, let us remember that our imperfections are not obstacles to our success but are essential elements of our unique story. They are what make us who we are, and it is in accepting and embracing them that we find our truest self. Let this chapter be a testament to the power of self-compassion and the beauty of a life lived authentically, imperfections included.

A Call for Self-Exploration and Growth

Chapter 12

As we end our narrative of "Belief, Fear, and Love," in our final chapter, we have reached a significant milestone. My life's journey through the highs and lows of basketball has been a testament to the transformative power of self-exploration and growth. This chapter is not just a call to action; it's an invitation to embark on a journey of profound self-discovery and personal evolution.

The essence of self-exploration lies in the willingness to delve into the depths of our being. It's about confronting the truths we've shied away from, challenging the narratives we've long accepted, and uncovering the layers of our identity that have remained hidden or suppressed. In my coaching career, I've seen how self-exploration can unleash a player's true potential, revealing strengths and abilities they never knew they had. It's about breaking free from the limitations we've imposed on ourselves, whether consciously or subconsciously.

Growth, in this context, is not merely about skill enhancement or achieving success. It's about expanding our understanding of ourselves and the world around us. It's a journey that demands resilience, as true growth often comes from facing and overcoming adversity. On the basketball court, growth is evident in a player who learns from their mistakes, who adapts and evolves, not just in their technique but in their mental and emotional approach to the game.

This chapter calls for an introspective approach to life, urging us to question, reflect, and seek deeper meaning in our experiences. It's about recognizing that growth is an ongoing process, not a destination. Every experience, every challenge, and every triumph is an opportunity for learning and development.

The journey of self-exploration and growth also involves embracing change. Change is an inevitable part of life, and how we respond to it shapes our path. In the dynamic world of basketball, adaptability is key. Players who embrace change, who are open to new strategies and ways of thinking, often find themselves at the forefront of success. Similarly, in life, being adaptable and open to change paves the way for growth and fulfillment.

Moreover, this journey calls for a shift in perspective. It's about viewing life's challenges not as obstacles but as catalysts for growth. This shift can be transformative, turning what might seem like insurmountable hurdles into stepping stones towards personal development. It fosters resilience, a quality that I've always prioritized in my coaching. Resilience is not just about bouncing back from setbacks; it's about growing stronger and wiser through them.

The Strength in Rest and Renewal

I want to emphasize a crucial lesson I've learned both on and off the court: the distinction between giving up and taking a moment to rest before forging ahead. This lesson has been a cornerstone in my philosophy, shaping not only my coaching strategies but also my approach to life's myriad challenges.

In the world of competitive sports, the pressure to continuously perform at peak levels can be overwhelming. Players often find themselves at a crossroad where fatigue, both mental and physical, beckons them to surrender. Yet, it is in these moments that the true essence of determination is tested. To give up means to accept defeat, to concede that the obstacles are insurmountable. However, to rest, to gather oneself, and to dive back into the fray is the hallmark of true resilience and determination.

This concept of rest and renewal is not about weakness or retreat; it's about wisdom and strategy. It's recognizing that sometimes, the path to victory involves a tactical pause, a moment to recharge and reassess. In my coaching sessions, I've often emphasized the importance of listening to one's body and mind. A player who understands the value of rest, who can step back momentarily to regain strength, returns to the game with renewed vigor and a clearer perspective.

The application of this principle extends beyond the basketball court. In life, we are constantly faced with challenges that test our resolve and endurance. The societal narrative often equates continuous struggle with strength, inadvertently glorifying the idea of pushing oneself to the brink of exhaustion. However, the art of achieving true growth and fulfillment lies in recognizing when to pause, reflect, and rejuvenate.

Resting and returning with renewed determination is a testament to one's inner strength. It's an acknowledgment that our journey is a marathon, not a sprint. It involves understanding that every challenge we face is an opportunity for growth, but only if we approach it with a clear mind and a rejuvenated spirit.

Moreover, this approach fosters self-compassion and mindfulness. It allows us to be kind to ourselves, to understand our limitations, and to approach our goals with a mindset that values our well-being as much as our achievements. This balanced approach is crucial for sustainable success and personal growth.

The Power of Self-Awareness in Personal Evolution

Self-awareness, a concept I've come to regard as the cornerstone of all personal growth, is the ability to observe and understand one's own thoughts, feelings, and behaviors. It's about recognizing your strengths, weaknesses, values, and beliefs, and using this understanding as a tool for meaningful changes in your life.

Self-awareness is a skill that I've not only cultivated in myself but have also endeavored to instill in every player I've coached. On the basketball court, self-aware players are those who understand their abilities and limitations, who can objectively analyze their performance, and who can adapt their strategies accordingly. This level of self-awareness is what transforms a good player into a great one.

Off the court, the importance of self-awareness becomes even more pronounced. It's the foundation upon which we build our relationships, make our career choices, and navigate the complexities of life. When we're self-aware, we're better equipped to make decisions that align with our true selves, rather than being swayed by fleeting emotions or external pressures.

One key aspect of self-awareness is the ability to recognize and embrace our imperfections. In a culture that often glorifies perfection, acknowledging our flaws can be a daunting task. However, it's in embracing these imperfections that we find our true strength. It's understanding that our flaws are part of what makes us unique, and that growth comes from recognizing and working on these areas.

Self-awareness also involves a deep understanding of our values and beliefs. It's about knowing what truly matters to us, what drives our actions, and what gives our life meaning. This understanding is crucial in making choices that bring us fulfillment and happiness. In my journey, both as a coach and an individual, understanding my core values has been key to making decisions that resonate with my true self.

Another important aspect of self-awareness is emotional intelligence. It's the ability to understand and manage our emotions, as well as to empathize with others. This emotional intelligence is vital in building strong relationships, both personally and professionally. It helps us communicate effectively, resolve conflicts, and connect with others on a deeper level.

In cultivating self-awareness, practices like mindfulness and reflection are invaluable. They allow us to pause, to observe our thoughts and feelings without judgment, and to gain insights into our inner workings. This mindful practice has been a game-changer for me and many of the athletes I've coached. It creates a space for growth, for understanding, and for transformation.

Summarizing the Forces of Belief, Fear, and Love

As we conclude our exploration of "Belief, Fear, and Love," it's essential to reflect on how these powerful forces have shaped not just my journey as Coach Ron Moncrief but also the human experience at large. These elements - belief, fear, and love - are not isolated entities; they intertwine and interact, profoundly influencing our personal development and life choices.

Belief has been a guiding light in my life, both on and off the court. It's the foundation upon which we build our perceptions of the world and ourselves. Belief fuels our aspirations, drives our actions, and shapes our reality. In basketball, belief is what empowers a player to attempt the game-winning shot or to push through physical and mental barriers. In life, belief steers our decisions, bolsters our courage in the face of adversity, and shapes our destiny. However, belief is not just about optimism; it's about grounding our hopes and dreams in reality, about having the conviction to pursue our goals while being adaptable and resilient.

Fear, on the other hand, is a double-edged sword. It's a natural and necessary part of the human condition, often serving as a protective mechanism. Yet, unbridled fear can become a barrier, holding us back from embracing new opportunities or realizing our full potential.

In my coaching career, I've seen how fear can manifest as performance anxiety or reluctance to take risks. In life, fear can hinder our personal growth, affect our relationships, and limit our experiences. Overcoming fear is not about eradicating it but about understanding and managing it, transforming it into a source of strength and wisdom.

Love is perhaps the most potent of all. It's the force that binds us, that drives us to care, to connect, and to create. In the context of basketball, love for the game is what motivates players to train relentlessly, to play with passion, and to support their teammates. In life, love influences our choices, shapes our relationships, and imparts meaning to our existence. However, love is more than just an emotion; it's an action, a commitment to others and to ourselves. It's about nurturing our relationships, fostering empathy, and striving to make a positive impact in the world.

The balance and interaction between belief, fear, and love are what make the human experience so rich and complex. Each of these forces influences the others in profound ways. Belief can overcome fear, fear can deepen our understanding of love, and love can reinforce our beliefs. This dynamic interplay is what drives our growth, shapes our character, and defines our journey through life.

In summarizing the roles of belief, fear, and love, it's clear that these forces are not static; they are dynamic and ever-evolving. They are the lenses through which we view the world and ourselves. As we navigate through life, the challenge is to find a harmonious balance between these forces, allowing them to guide us towards a path of self-discovery, resilience, and fulfillment.

Encouraging Personal Reflection and Inner Evolution

Personal reflection is the art of looking inward, of examining our thoughts, feelings, and motivations with honesty and openness. It's about understanding the 'why' behind what we do, not just the 'what.' In my coaching, I've always stressed the importance of this introspective process. It's one thing to teach a player the mechanics of a perfect shot, but it's another to instill in them the self-awareness that helps them understand their reactions under pressure, their resilience in the face of defeat, and their ability to celebrate their victories with humility.

The journey of inner evolution is continuous and requires a commitment to growth and self-improvement. It's about recognizing that who we are today is not who we have to be tomorrow. We are all works in progress, capable of learning, adapting, and evolving. This process is not linear; it involves setbacks and breakthroughs, each offering valuable lessons.

I advocate for ongoing self-reflection as a tool for personal evolution. It's through this process that we come to understand our strengths and weaknesses, our fears and aspirations. Self-reflection helps us navigate the complex terrain of our emotions and thoughts, allowing us to make more informed and authentic decisions.

Encouraging practices that foster personal evolution is also essential. This could involve mindfulness techniques, journaling, or simply dedicating time for quiet contemplation. In my life, I've found that even a few moments of introspection before a game or after a practice session can offer clarity and insight.

This chapter, therefore, is an invitation to each reader to engage in their journey of self-exploration and growth. It's a call to embrace the ever-evolving nature of our existence, to recognize the power of introspection in understanding ourselves, and to commit to practices that enhance our personal evolution.

As we navigate our paths, let us remember that self-awareness is a powerful guide. It illuminates our strengths, reveals our weaknesses, and offers a roadmap for continuous growth. Let's embrace this journey with an open heart and a willing spirit, knowing that the journey itself is as important as the destination.

The Power of Self-Awareness in Navigating Life

In this final chapter, "A Call for Self-Exploration and Growth," we delved into the profound impact of self-awareness in our lives. This journey, which I have navigated through both my coaching career and personal experiences, highlights the transformative role of self-awareness in finding meaning, purpose, and fulfillment. The call for self-awareness is not just a directive to change who we are but rather an invitation to deeply understand, embrace, and authentically be ourselves.

Self-awareness, in my view, is like a beacon of light guiding us back to our true selves. It's about recognizing our inner strengths and weaknesses, understanding our values and beliefs, and being mindful of how our thoughts and actions shape our lives. In the fast-paced and often externally-driven world of competitive basketball, cultivating self-awareness has been crucial for both my players and myself. It has empowered us to make decisions rooted in our core values rather than being swayed by external pressures or fleeting emotions.

The journey towards self-awareness is indeed challenging, but the rewards are immeasurable.

It enables us to live more purposefully, aligning our actions with our true selves. As a coach, I've witnessed the profound growth that players experience when they engage in self-reflection. They learn to play not just with their physical abilities but with their hearts and minds, bringing a level of authenticity and passion to the game that transcends the physical aspects.

In our lives, self-awareness helps us navigate the complexities of our relationships, career choices, and personal goals. It allows us to face life's challenges with a deeper understanding of ourselves, enhancing our ability to adapt, grow, and thrive. Moreover, self-awareness fosters resilience - the ability to bounce back from setbacks and view challenges as opportunities for growth.

One key aspect of developing self-awareness is embracing our imperfections. In a society that often glorifies perfection, acknowledging and accepting our flaws can be a powerful step towards authenticity. It's about understanding that our imperfections are part of our unique journey, contributing to our growth and making us who we are.

Cultivating self-awareness also involves recognizing the beauty and learning in every step of our journey. It's about finding value in each experience, whether it's a triumphant win or a humbling loss. This perspective fosters self-compassion, allowing us to treat ourselves with kindness and understanding, which in turn enhances our personal growth.

To encourage this journey of self-reflection and inner evolution, I advocate for practices such as mindfulness, journaling, and open dialogue. These practices provide us with the tools to explore our inner world, gain insights into our thoughts and emotions, and develop a deeper connection with ourselves.

In conclusion, Chapter 12 serves as a powerful reminder of the importance of self-awareness in our lives. It's a call to embark on a journey of self-exploration and growth, to embrace the beauty in our imperfections, and to find fulfillment in being our truest selves. The path to self-awareness may be strewn with challenges, but the clarity, purpose, and inner peace it brings are the hallmarks of a life well-lived. Let us all heed this call, for it is in knowing ourselves that we unlock the full potential of our existence.

A Last Word From The Author

As the final words of this book are penned, I reflect upon the journey we've embarked upon together through these pages. "Belief, Fear, and Love: The Brutal Truth of How I Have Learned All

Three of These Have Shaped Our Lives and Choices" is more than just a narrative; it's a part of my soul, a collection of life lessons gleaned from the basketball court and beyond.

This book was born from a lifetime of experiences, a voyage through the tumultuous seas of triumph and defeat, joy and sorrow, certainty and doubt. My career in coaching women's basketball has been more than a profession; it has been a platform for profound personal and communal growth. The court became a microcosm of the larger world, where belief, fear, and love constantly played out, influencing decisions, shaping destinies.

Belief, as I have learned, is the bedrock upon which we build our lives. It's a powerful force that shapes our perception, fuels our passion, and drives us toward our goals. Yet, it's also a delicate entity, vulnerable to the storms of doubt and change. In this book, I've shared how belief can be both a beacon of hope and a blindfold of delusion, steering us through the darkness and sometimes leading us astray.

Fear, the ever-present shadow, has been a constant companion on this journey. It's a force that can paralyze the strongest of us, clouding our judgment and stifling our potential. Yet, in facing our fears, in acknowledging and confronting them, we find the keys to freedom and growth. This book has been my attempt to demystify fear, to transform it from a formidable foe into a source of strength and wisdom.

Love, the most potent and enigmatic of all, has been the ultimate driving force in my life. It's the glue that binds us, the light that guides us, and the energy that propels us forward. In coaching, love for the game, for the players, and for the journey has been my guiding principle. This book encapsulates the various facets of love - its power to heal, to unite, and to transform.

As you, the reader, turn the final pages of this book, my hope is that you take away more than just stories and insights. I hope this book serves as a mirror, reflecting your own experiences and beliefs, fears and loves. I hope it acts as a compass, guiding you toward a path of introspection, self-awareness, and growth.

The journey of self-exploration is never-ending. As we evolve, so do our beliefs, our fears, and our capacity to love. This book is an invitation to continue that journey, to dive deeper into the depths of your being, to confront the truths you've shied away from, and to embrace the totality of your existence.

Remember, the strength to grow and evolve lies within you. It's in the quiet moments of reflection, in the courageous steps taken in the face of fear, and in the love that we share with the world. May this book be a catalyst for your own journey of self-discovery and evolution.

Thank you for sharing this journey with me. May your path be illuminated with belief, fortified with courage, and enriched with love.

With Gratitude,

Coach Ron Moncrief.

www.ingramcontent.com/pod-product-compliance
Lightning Source LLC
LaVergne TN
LVHW031611060526
838201LV00065B/4808